D1593979

An Angel
on my Shoulder

The Biography of
E. Claiborne Robins

Juliet E. Shield

Opa Publishing
Aspen, Colorado

Copyright © 1995 by Juliet E. Shield

Published by Opa Publishing

Unless otherwise stated, all photographs
were obtained from A. H. Robins Archives

Edited by: Juliet E. Shield and Paul Andersen
Design by: Juliet E. Shield and Frank Gayer Martin

Library of Congress Cataloging-in-Publication Data

Shield, Juliet E.
An Angel on my Shoulder:
The Biography of E. Claiborne Robins
ISBN: 0-9647846-0-2
Library of Congress Catalog Card Number: 95-70791

First Printing

Printed in the United States of America

To order copies of this book write to
Opa Publishing, P.O. Box 1349, Aspen, Colorado, 81612;
or fax: 970-925-6868; or e-mail: OpaPublish@aol.com

*For my family
in loving memory
of my grandfather*

*Edwin Claiborne Robins
July 8, 1910 – July 6, 1995*

CONTENTS

FOREWORD

For many years I had entertained the thought of writing an autobiography. I have had a remarkable life and a number of experiences that few, if any other, people in the world have been fortunate to achieve. Were it not for the encouragement and at times insistence of my granddaughter, Juliet Elizabeth Shield, my biography would probably not have been written. For her untiring efforts in bringing this book to fruition I owe her a deep debt of gratitude.

E. Claiborne Robins

ACKNOWLEDGEMENTS

First and most importantly, I want to thank my grandfather, E. Claiborne Robins, for allowing me to delve into his life, his thoughts, his remembrances, his philosophies, and for providing me with the source material to write such a complete and inspiring biography. Thanks to my grandmother, Lora McGlasson Robins, for her unwavering support of my desire to write this book, and for the information she provided to my grandfather and me in recalling events. Thanks to my mother, Elizabeth Robins Porter, for her faith that I could accomplish whatever I set my mind to, for all her help and support with the project, and for being "her daughter." Thanks to my aunt, Ann Carol Robins Marchant and my uncle, E. Claiborne Robins, Jr. whose quotes and information helped enrich the book. Thanks to my partner in life, J. David Taylor, for listening to hours of taped material, supporting me through periods of frustration and discouragement, and for giving me feedback on seemingly endless revisions. Thanks to the A. H. Robins employees I interviewed who helped add some wonderful anecdotes to the story. Thanks to Randy Walker, whose invaluable assistance with months of interviewing my grandfather and others, provided me with a wider range of material than I could have obtained without him. Thanks to Frank Martin for helping me with the design and layout of the book, and for his willingness to work with me in the evenings and on weekends. And finally many thanks to Paul Andersen, my editor, without whom I would not have been able to accomplish this project. Together we broke new ground; this was the first book for both of us. The task seemed overwhelming at first, but because of Paul's energy and skill, we mutually fueled each other's enthusiasm to complete this fascinating compendium of my grandfather's life.

INTRODUCTION

At my birth in Richmond in 1961, the A. H. Robins Company had reached $40 million in sales, and my grandfather, E. Claiborne Robins, was a prominent civic leader. My mother, Betty, was the eldest of his three children and she expressed a sense of devotion to him that made me want to know more about the man who had such an influence on her.

My mother, father, and I lived the first two years of my life in Virginia while my father finished college, and then we moved to Hanover, New Hampshire where he attended graduate school at The Amos Tuck School at Dartmouth. When my parents separated, I stayed in New England with my mother who loved the area. As a child it seemed like we were a world away from the rest of my family — both Shield and Robins — in Richmond. This distance though, was greater than just the miles between us, as I was to learn later when I was teasingly called a "Yankee" by the southern loyalists in the family.

In December of 1968 and 1969, when I was 7 and 8 years old, I would come in from skiing and thaw out my cold feet in front of the fire at the Pico Peak ski lodge in Vermont. My mother had remarried and was working a few steps away at the ski school counter. Nearby, I remember there was a large black and white Chap Stick tube illuminated in an advertisement. I knew that this was my Grandaddy's ad and felt proud that his was one of the few displayed. Although I didn't spend very much time with my grandparents, I felt more connected somehow when I looked at that ad.

I visited Richmond a couple of times a year, sometimes to see my father and the Shield family, and on other occasions to visit Virginia Beach with the Robins family. My grandparents always

Juliet stands between her grandparents, Lora and Claiborne (with sister Robin at right) at a family gathering in 1968.

greeted me with a "Hi Dawlin" and a big hug, and I always looked forward to the trips to the beach to see them. Granddaddy would swim with us in the pool and help us watch for dolphins out the big picture window that looked up and down the oceanfront. Grandmommy would cook our favorite fried chicken and spend time collecting shells with us on the beach. Grandchildren and grandparents have a special bond, a shared unconditional love, and I was very lucky to know them all.

In my teens I became aware of more Robins products as I recognized the Robins logo with its green and black colors. Whenever I visited a drugstore I would search out the appropriate aisle to make sure that all of the Robitussin and Chap Stick products were prominently displayed, something I unconsciously do even today. Once when I was in England I went into an apothecary just to see if any products were sold there. I found Dimetapp, spelled in the English version, Dimotapp. Another time I even moved a competitor's product to the rear so that Chap Stick would be more visible. No doubt I have always been biased concerning my choice of lip balm. My friends are either amused or must think I'm a pest as I extol the virtues of Chap Stick if they pull out a competitor's product. I was already an A. H. Robins salesperson from the time I was a child and didn't even know it.

As I came of age, my curiosity about my family and the need to reconnect compelled me to return to Virginia. I first moved back when I decided to attend my grandfather's alma mater, the University of Richmond. During my freshman year I spent a lot of time with my Virginia family and was glad to be a part of celebrations that I had missed throughout my childhood. Also, during this time I became aware of the extended "Robins family" that existed at the company. Although I went on to graduate from Bucknell University in Pennsylvania in 1983, I decided once again to return to Richmond. The intrigue and attraction of this company family motivated me to find out about it by working for the company.

In 1984 I met with Executive Vice President Robert Watts and together we designed an internship whereby I would work in several departments in the company over the course of the year. I worked in the Consumer Products Division, the Order Depart-

Juliet (right) at her college graduation party with Claiborne and Lora and friend, Karen Fracas, in 1983. The party, "Juliet's June Jubilee," was hosted by Claiborne and Lora at their home, Clear View.

ment, and Personnel. All three departments allowed me to get a taste of the company's operations as well as a chance to get to know a wide range of Robins employees.

In August 1985 — only a month after the company filed for bankruptcy in chapter 11 — I became a full-time employee taking a position in the sales field in Richmond. Representing A. H. Robins in one of the most important capacities, much like my grandfather had fifty years before, I called on physicians and dentists to sell/detail our products. In most cases I was welcomed with open arms as local doctors wanted to show their support for the company and tell me what a tragedy it was that we were forced into Chapter 11. OB-GYN's in Richmond told me that they personally had few, if any, problems with the Dalkon Shield. Instead of feeling embarrassed when I called on them, I felt proud.

This was a difficult period for the family with the uncertainty of the company's future. We knew it was possible that the stock would eventually be worthless. At the company, the big question in everyone's mind was who is going to purchase the business and will we still have that family feeling when the new owner takes command? Throughout this difficult period between 1985-1989, the employees of the company were incredibly optimistic, loyal and unified. In every department I met wonderful people who were very supportive.

In 1987, after 2 1/2 years in the field, I moved to the International Division — the department in the company where I had strived to be all along. My position was Marketing Assistant to Manager Steve McGuffin. I regularly corresponded with our foreign offices and subsidiaries, and I designed and wrote the new Product Compendium.

My duties also enabled me to travel to a few of our European subsidiaries including A. H. Robins in England, and Georg A. Brenner in Germany. I enjoyed meeting our foreign personnel and they seemed to enjoy meeting me, not only as a representative from the home office, but as the granddaughter of Claiborne

Robins, for whom they had tremendous respect.

Some of my most gratifying days at A. H. Robins, however, were during the spring of 1988 when my Uncle Claiborne asked me to prepare a presentation for my grandparents' 50th wedding anniversary. Working together with former advertising employee, Frank Mann, who ran his own media consulting firm, we orchestrated the celebration for June 24. The party was to be the culmination of a successful marriage and business and therefore the project was a labor of love from the start.

I enjoyed playing the sleuth as I gathered old photographs and films from Clear View's basement and discreetly questioned my grandparents for information about their early life together. Interviewing many longtime employees and retirees including Marshall Phillips, Johnny Gordon, Vangie Windsor, Georgette Tignor, Mallory Freeman, Helen Payne, Eddy Morton, Carlton Gammon, Happy Holloway, Grayson Kirtland, and Burwell Robinson, I gathered anecdotes to include in the presentation. I also made a quick trip to Texas to gather information about my grandmother's family and to get photographs of the places where they spent time together in 1937 when they met.

On the evening of the party I felt proud as we presented our multimedia film of their life together. My grandmother called me a "rascal" for surprising her, and everyone in the family enjoyed the show, but I knew that a twenty minute presentation barely scratched the surface. A book would be yet another avenue to better connect with my roots.

Initially I wanted to explore the entire story of the Robins family history in America starting with John Robins of Gloucester, VA, who was given a 2000 acre land grant by King James I in 1640. Needless to say, as I realized the scope of this project, I pared it down to my grandfather's biography.

With all my eagerness, however, my grandfather wasn't convinced until the summer of 1992 that his life story was worth telling. I'm glad he finally agreed to be interviewed because now his philosophies and values will not be lost. Using his quotes wherever possible, I wanted the reader to know the man through his own words. Future generations of the family will now have a sense of history through his eyes and know what a fine human being he was.

January 20, 1995
Aspen, Colorado

Just as this book was going to print my grandfather died after a brief illness. He had been diagnosed with pancreatic cancer only three weeks prior to his death and mercifully did not suffer any pain. The notes that the family has received have reaffirmed how much E. Claiborne Robins was respected and loved. He will be greatly missed by those of us who had the privilege of knowing him.

July 17, 1995

I

CASCARA

When spring comes to the University of Richmond, the lakeside campus blooms with white and pink dogwood, azalea, and a chorus of bird song. Students rush back and forth from classes, feeling excitement at the end of another school year and at the prospect of a rejuvenating summer break.

As one strolls around the campus it becomes obvious to the visitor that E. Claiborne Robins and his family are particularly devoted to the University of Richmond. To the side of the campus sits the Robins Center, the large athletic facility built by Claiborne and his children. This multi-million dollar gift is only one part of a legacy of contributions that Claiborne has made to his alma mater. Other buildings that display the family name include Robins Hall, named in honor of his mother, Martha Taylor Robins; Lora Robins Court; Lora Robins Gallery; and the E. Claiborne Robins School of Business.

Claiborne would be the last person to boast about his achievements or his unprecedented $50 million gift to the university in 1969, the largest gift of its time given by an individual to a private university. Philanthropy has long been one of Claiborne's primary satisfactions in life. To friends, family and employees of the A. H. Robins Company who know him, Claiborne's philanthropy is predicated on a sincere spirit of caring, a genuine humanity. E. Claiborne Robins is revered in Richmond and elsewhere, not only for his many cash gifts and endowments, but also for the warmth of his personal relationships.

To one friend, he is a "prince of philanthropy." To his children, he is a strong guiding influence. To his community, he is a fine example of Southern gentility and an unwavering practitioner of the golden rule. To the hundreds of people whose lives he has touched, through business and civic duties, he is an exemplar of hard work, commitment, dedication and the value of education.

The sum of Claiborne's life is as much a story of personal drive and success as it is the story of a benefactor whose first concern was always for the people around him. Yet humility and a strong sense of faith cause Claiborne to attribute the successes of his life to the influence of the individuals who nurtured him and to the powers that be that have guided him.

The Robins family name has been known in Richmond, Virginia for well over a century and Claiborne's prominence within his community can be traced to the A. H. Robins Company, the family enterprise he built from practically nothing into a billion dollar concern. For E. Claiborne Robins, the story begins with his grandfather.

Albert Hartley Robins, late 1800s.

Albert Hartley Robins was born in Virginia in 1842 and apprenticed at the Richmond apothecary of Meade & Baker until the Civil War broke out in 1861. At 19 years of age Albert joined the Richmond Grays of the First Virginia Regiment, and after two years of service was wounded at the Battle of Brandy Station, Virginia in the largest cavalry battle of the Civil War.

Although Albert's skull was grazed by a shell, he recovered quickly and rejoined the Confederate war effort to secede Virginia and the Confederacy from the Union. In 1864 Albert was captured by Union forces at the Battle of Sayler Creek along with 6,000 other Confederate troops in a major Union victory. The outcome of that battle caused Confederate General Robert E. Lee to question a subordinate as to whether his entire army had been vanquished that day.

In an interview printed in the *Richmond Times-Dispatch* on

CASCARA

December 25, 1934, Albert — at 92 years of age — recalled a Christmas dinner during the war. Albert was a private in the company of Confederate infantry of which a certain Bob Mayo of Richmond was first lieutenant. Albert remembered, "A few of us were able to get hold of a pretty good cut of fresh beef. We took it back to camp with us and prepared for a feast. When we got the fire ready, however, we found that our beef didn't have enough fat either for cooking or gravy. It looked as though our little Christmas party was going to be  spoiled after all, until one of the boys happened to remember that on the night before he had seen two tallow candles in Bob Mayo's desk in his tent.

Albert Hartley Robins at age 92 in 1934.

"So we drew straws between the six of us to see who the petty thief would be. I was elected. Those two candles did the trick for us in great style, and all of us had enough fine, brown gravy for our cornbread that day. But Mayo was hopping mad that night when he got back and found his candles gone. Candles were almost as difficult to get as turkey, and he did his best to find out who had taken them. I never told him until after the war ... what actually became of those candles, and we both had a big laugh over it."

When the Civil War ended in 1865, Albert was determined to resume his work in pharmaceuticals. His own suffering during the war and the haunting misery of his wounded comrades convinced him of the need for pharmaceuticals. Albert opened an apothecary in war-torn Richmond in 1866, a year after

Appomattox, hanging a shingle advertising medicinal chemicals.

Effective medicines were in great need during the war as soldiers suffered amputations without anesthesia, died of gangrene, and were cut down by fevers and other illnesses for which there were no medicines. Most drug stores sold products that had little scientific basis and often bordered on alchemy.

Asafetida, a fetid gum resin from oriental plants, was popular at the time as a prophylactic against disease, and children wore bottles of it around their necks to ward off illness. Such so-called remedies were sold as cures for everything from colds to cancers, but the claims of certain cures were greatly exaggerated. Understanding a real need for effective cures, Albert dedicated himself to the pharmaceutical business with a strict commitment to providing only quality medicines.

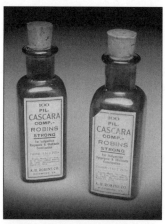

Because he sold only those products that had a proven record, "Doc Robins," as he was soon known, became one of the most respected pharmacists in Richmond. Albert's most successful product was Robins Cascara Compound, which he recommended for, "Indigestion, Dyspepsia & Obstinate Constipation."

Albert made the little black pills himself, rolling them by hand in the

Robins Cascara Compound.

back room of his pharmacy. Customers came from all over the city to buy the pills at Robins' Pharmacy. By the 1890s sales of Cascara pills had begun to grow, and the Robins name became known throughout Richmond.

In the photographs for which he posed, Albert wore the stern and formidable look of a serious businessman, but it was known that Albert loved people. He was regarded fondly for the hospitality he showered on the many Robins relatives visiting from Gloucester, and King and Queen counties of Virginia.

To expand his successful business and provide more room for his legions of guests, Albert moved the Robins Pharmacy to 200 E. Marshall Street in 1891. "My business is halfway between the poorhouse and the penitentiary," Albert would joke, "but I hope to stay out of both." This he did, and as his fortunes grew, his properties included a guest house, the main house and the apothecary.

Albert Hartley Robins.

"People in those days went in a great deal more for visiting from home to home than they do now, and we put a little more store by hospitality," Albert said in the interview with the *Richmond Times-Dispatch* in 1934.

An enterprising man, Albert gave his life's energy to a business that required his attention almost seven days a week. Other than church activities, he took part in few, if any, civic endeavors. When Albert finally retired from the pharmacy business in 1929 he was 87 and had profited from a distinguished career of 63 years.

In the style of the day, Albert's store on East Marshall had a center aisle with large, glass showcases on either side. A handsome interior balcony curved around the walls and was used mostly for surplus stock. In the back of the store Albert made many of his own drug compounds. To accommodate his large vanilla business, Albert crushed vanilla beans for extract. He stocked some sundry products, but mostly he focused on prescriptions.

A newspaper advertisement for Robins Pharmacy from the turn of the century offered "flavoring extracts, essences, spices, soap, perfumery and toilet requisites," along with "the best steel enameled, rubber and glass goods for your sick." Albert even dispensed information on what gifts would be appropriate for the

The original Robins' Pharmacy established by Albert Hartley Robins, in Richmond, Virginia in 1866.

browsing medical students who frequented his store. Attesting to his serious nature, however, there was no soda fountain and never would be at his apothecary.

Once his business was thriving, Albert married Jane F. Heywood, who became known in the family as Nanny. They had four children, including Claiborne, who was born in 1873. Claiborne was educated in Richmond and took an early interest in his father's business, graduating from what later became the Medical College of Virginia in 1896 with the highest grade in the class.

Claiborne pursued the family business and worked hard to fit the shoes of his dedicated father. After college, however, Claiborne determined that pharmaceutical products should be promoted directly to doctors, and he began "detailing" the benefits of Robins' products to Richmond doctors in hopes they would prescribe his line of drugs to their patients.

Father and son disagreed on each others' approach, but they carried out their businesses side by side. Albert ran the apothecary downstairs while Claiborne mailed out medications in an office upstairs.

Claiborne formed the A. H. Robins Company in 1896 and, like Albert, his leading product was Cascara. Claiborne purchased several hundred thousand Cascara pills from Sharp and Dohme — later Merck, Sharp, and Dohme — and shipped them out to pharmacies on orders he filled through traveling sales.

While Albert remained in Richmond and sold his products over the counter, Claiborne took to the road by train, horse and buggy, or even by foot, to tell the Robins story to doctors throughout the region. The first few years of the A. H. Robins Company were somewhat difficult, but Claiborne was determined to make a success of it.

Travel became a big part of Claiborne's life at the turn of the century and he was away

Claiborne Robins, circa 1902.

from home for long periods of time. "In those days it took eight hours to get to Washington," said E. Claiborne of the drives his father made on country roads threading through Ashland and Fredericksburg. "If it rained, the roads almost became impassable. I remember going up to Washington, and it was an all-day trip. This was in the teens. I think the first paved roads to Washington were in 1925-1927."

Claiborne enjoyed his mobility and the opportunity to detail Robins products to physicians in Virginia, North Carolina, and parts of Tennessee. It was on a train trip to Tennessee that he met his future wife.

Martha Taylor, the daughter of a gentleman farmer from Rutherford, Tennessee, was on her way home by train from New York, where she had been studying piano. Reading a book, she looked up and saw a young man smiling at her.

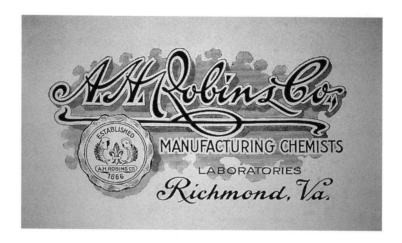

Claiborne, who was traveling for his company, was smitten by the pretty young lady. The custom of the day dictated that a proper lady did not respond to advances made by men on public transportation, especially traveling salesmen. Claiborne prevailed, however, and they struck up a conversation.

Claiborne learned that Martha's heart-felt interest was music, which was also his love, and she found herself drawn to the handsome young man. Their chance meeting opened the door for a serious courtship, and after writing her family for permission to pay a call, Claiborne visited Martha several times at her home in Rutherford.

"He apparently had a very gracious personality," said E. Claiborne, "and all the relatives were just crazy about my father. They thought he was the greatest thing ever put on this earth. He evidently was charming, but he also loved music and, of course, that was one of her great loves. When he was on the road traveling for the company, which he was the time that he met her, my father used to send her sheet music."

Martha had shown such talent at the piano at an early age that, by 18, her teachers recommended that she study under the noted composer, pianist, and teacher, Professor Raffaele Joseffy, of N. Tarrytown, New York.

Martha traveled to New York for an audition, one of her first excursions away from home and a formidable trip for a young lady. When she arrived at Joseffy's house, her knock on the door was answered by a stern-looking man who asked her to come in, sit down at the piano, and play.

"Play anything that comes to your mind," said Joseffy. Dutifully, and with nerves tightly wound, Martha obliged. She played a tune that she loved and thought appropriate for this noteworthy musician. She had not gotten more than half a minute into the piece before Joseffy said, "Stop!"

"Oh, my, that's the end of the line," thought Martha, and she burst into tears.

"What are you crying for?" asked Joseffy.

"Why, I've obviously failed," said the teary-eyed girl.

"Don't be stupid," scolded Joseffy. "I've already decided to take you."

Thus began Martha Taylor's two years of study with Professor Joseffy.

Martha was returning home after finishing her instruction when she met Claiborne. During two years of courtship the couple fell in love. They were married in 1906. Martha left Rutherford for Richmond and joined Claiborne in his company work, giving up a promising musical career to help her husband with his pharmaceutical business. Her new life with Claiborne meant the sacrifice of her aspiration to become a concert pianist.

With Claiborne's marketing skills the A. H. Robins Company began to grow. By 1912 sales grossed nearly $25,000, with $5,000 in net profits. Home life had

Claiborne Robins in 1910.

Martha Taylor Robins, circa 1930s.

brought joy to Claiborne and Martha. He sold pharmaceuticals and she kept the accounts. A baby boy, Albert, was born in 1908 and another son, Edwin Claiborne, was born in 1910.

The family suffered a tragedy, however, when son Albert died of a childhood illness. Then in 1912, Claiborne fell ill to endocarditis, an inflammation of the lining of the heart attributed to poor dental care. The disease, which modern antibiotics can now easily cure, proved fatal, and Claiborne Robins, founder of the A. H. Robins Company, died of heart failure at 39. He left behind his father, a grieving widow, and a sole heir, his two-year-old son, Edwin Claiborne Robins.

Martha Taylor quickly showed herself a capable woman. Buoyed by determination and a deep inner strength, she decided to keep the small family company going and remain in Richmond. She plunged into the business, filling orders and meeting the needs of the clientele her husband had established. Through her industry and fortitude she somehow coped with the loss of her husband, struggled to maintain a source of income, and managed to raise her son.

Albert Hartley Robins was 73 at the time of his son's death and was unable to offer Martha much more than moral support in carrying on without Claiborne. This propelled Martha into the role of pharmaceutical manufacturer, which, in 1912, made her one of very few women in the South to enter the world of business.

The demands on her time forced her to surrender any remaining ambition as a pianist. Instead of practicing arpeggios she took charge of the household and filled orders in the upstairs office. She soon hired two employees and moved to more spacious quarters on Sixth Street.

"Of course she inherited this very small business, which she knew nothing about," said her son, Claiborne. "She had a great deal of courage and worked very hard to maintain it. She didn't know enough about it to expand it. She tried putting on some detailmen after my father's death, but the selection was not the best, and she finally just had to let them go because they weren't producing enough to justify their maintenance. From that point on she did a little bit of direct mail and a little bit of sampling by mail, but she didn't have the funds or know-how to expand."

With his father gone and his mother immersed in a struggling business, Claiborne grew up in a rapidly changing world that held immediate challenges.

II

MENTORS

In 1912, at the time of Claiborne's father's death, Richmond had a population of 127,000 and was growing in commerce and culture. The Jefferson Hotel was reputed to be the finest in the South, charging $1.50 a day and up for its rooms. Citizens paid $2.25 to $5.00 a day for a stay in Richmond's hospitals. Woodrow Wilson launched his campaign for the presidency from Richmond that year, speaking at Richmond College, the General Assembly, and the City Auditorium.

Richmond College was located on West Grace Street. The Richmond Female Institute, the forerunner of the Women's College, was on East Marshall, and would later become Westhampton College. Claiborne was ten when Richmond College, Westhampton College, and the T. C. Williams School of Law merged to become the University of Richmond.

Claiborne relied on two remarkable mentors in his early life, his mother, Martha Taylor Robins, and his teacher, John Peyton McQuire. "Between John Peyton McQuire and my dear mother, I guess that's where I got my influences," Claiborne said.

Martha Taylor Robins in 1942.

The boy's earliest view of life evolved primarily from the influence of his mother. As primary care giver, she was there from the beginning, nursing her child through illness, cradling his head in sleep, and, as he matured, introducing him to an ever-expanding world. As the head of her small family, Martha Taylor Robins became both parent and provider.

"My mother had a tragic life in so many ways," reflected Claiborne, "with the death of her husband in 1912 and the death of her first son, who died either before I was born or very shortly after. She had the death of her husband and the death of her son in about four years. In a way, I was the only child, which, I must say in looking back — I'm probably selfish — but in some ways it's a blessing and in some ways it's a curse. It would be good to have brothers and sisters; on the other hand, not having any competition is sometimes not too bad."

Martha and her two-year-old son were comfortable in their home on Park Avenue, but Albert, her father-in-law, persuaded Martha to move downtown to live with him and Nanny. In addition to having his family under one roof, Albert received the benefit of the congenial Martha, who acted as his hostess in entertaining an increasing number of relatives.

The six-bedroom guest house, next door to the main house, was usually full of visitors who came to stay a few days, but sometimes stayed on for two or three weeks. It was not unusual to have several sittings for breakfast, where Martha served heaping platters of sausage, bacon, ham, eggs fixed two or three ways, spoonbread or toast, salty fish, fruits, and juices.

"He was a great one for entertaining relatives," said Claiborne. "There was always a swarm of relatives. He even had a house next door, a guest house, just for the relatives. We were in the main house; the guests all ate their meals at the main house. My mother was the one who planned the meals and supervised and ran the house, and so forth."

A full house sometimes disappointed Claiborne, who was

relegated to the third sitting in deference to guests whose comfort was given priority under his grandfather's gracious code of southern hospitality. Albert thrived on hosting family and friends, but his open house greatly increased Martha's duties. After almost a decade of living under the same roof, Martha felt compelled to move into her own home, and began looking for a suitable location.

"Well, after a little of that she got pretty sick of it, obviously, with so many relatives constantly there. They would come to stay three days and they would stay three weeks. Relatives came from Gloucester and King and Queen, and there were a lot of Robins down there at Gloucester. One thing is that it was so hard to travel in those days I guess they thought when they made the effort to come to Richmond they wanted to stay a little while. Nobody ever asked them to go home, so they stayed as long as they wanted. But my grandfather ... that apparently was his great joy in life, because other than working, he never traveled to speak of."

In downtown Richmond during Claiborne's early years Broad Street was a shopping area for ladies, while Main Street's financial district was generally frequented by men. Grace and Franklin Streets lay between the two business centers and were mostly residential.

Claiborne bought ice cream at Hellstern's on Seventh and Broad Streets, and his mother bought her meats, vegetables, pastries, and flowers at the old Sixth Street Market. There were fewer than 200 automobiles on the streets of Richmond in 1910, but more than 30 theaters flourished. Shopping and a variety of entertainment, along with family ties, drew Robins relatives to Richmond.

Claiborne was fascinated by his grandfather's apothecary where Albert sold Cuticura soap, which came three to the box. Albert, then in his 70s, gave Claiborne the empty boxes to use as building blocks, and the youngster enjoyed playing with them as much as any expensive toy.

Albert Hartley in front of his pharmacy at 200 East Marshall Street with his two-year-old grandson, E. Claiborne, in 1912.

When he was older, Claiborne was allowed to help in the apothecary waiting on customers if no technical information was needed. Occasionally, Albert gave his grandson prescriptions to give to customers, even allowing him to collect the money. Claiborne sometimes delivered prescriptions a few blocks away. During this time, Albert's first wife, Nanny, died. Albert later married Nanny's sister, Sally B. Heywood, whose nickname was Laddy.

At age seven or eight, while still living with his grandfather, Claiborne's interest in making money sharpened. "I could truthfully say that I have always had a desire to earn my own way, at least a part of my own way," recalled Claiborne. "The fact that my mother was of modest means, but who was very dedicated to seeing that I got a good education, made me want to help at the earliest possible years."

Claiborne knew he could make money as a newspaper boy, like the other children in town, so he began selling newspapers at Third and Broad Streets. He was selling newspapers a few feet away from the spot where Central National Bank, later Central Fidelity Bank, would one day build a skyscraper and invite him to serve on their board of directors. The shadows of an illustrious future were already cast on the young boy who began his business career selling the *Richmond News Leader* at five cents apiece from a canvas sack.

"My grandfather's house, where he had his apothecary at Second and Marshall, was only four blocks from the newspaper plant," said Claiborne. "I sold the *News Leader* because it was the afternoon paper. You just went back to the side door and paid for the number you wanted in cash. You paid 'em up front. I would pick up the papers from the plant — around 50 of them. I paid three cents and made two for every one sold.

"Third and Broad was not then considered a good location. It was sort of the only option that was available," explained Claiborne. "All the bigger guys had all the choice spots. If you went to any of the other corners they would beat you up because they were twice as big as I was. I made a dollar a day, which wasn't anything great, but in those days it was a lot more than now by a long shot. If you made a dollar in an afternoon, it was real money. That was my first stint at private enterprise."

Claiborne liked the jingling of coins in his pocket, and his mother encouraged him to be frugal by putting most of his money into a savings account. He kept a few cents for ice cream or candy, and kept his eyes open for other ventures. When another boy told Claiborne that he could make a lot of money selling magazines, he rode his bike over to the office of the Curtis Publishing Company and applied for a route.

"How many copies do you want?" asked the manager, sizing up the ambitious young salesman. Optimistically, Claiborne took a few copies of each magazine distributed by Curtis. Soon he was one of the leaders in magazine sales for the firm.

"I started out very small, and as I built it up I bought a little more and more ... no credit for anybody, everybody did cash. I got some regular customers; I delivered those by bicycle on a monthly basis. Of course, the ones that sold the most were *Ladies Home Journal* and *Saturday Evening Post.* They gave us a little more profit on *Country Gentleman,* as I recall, so I pushed that," he chuckled. "I did really well considering that I was selling farm magazines to city people."

Ladies Home Journal and *Saturday Evening Post* sold more easily, but the 12-year-old soon built up the *Country Gentleman* sales as his bread and butter. "That was strictly constructed for farmers," said Claiborne. "Why anybody in Richmond would ever buy it, I don't know, except for sympathy. Maybe they just wanted to help a little fellow out."

When Claiborne was ten, his mother, Martha, tired of the combined burden of hosting at Albert's home and of running the A. H. Robins Company, decided to focus on the business. Therefore, in 1920, she moved with Claiborne to 2412 Rosewood Avenue, a pleasant location near Byrd Park. It proved to be an excellent choice, with good neighbors who later helped Claiborne find work opportunities, travel adventures and even an early romantic interest.

As he grew older and more independent, Claiborne's motivation increased, and he showed promise as a salesman. At age 13 he did so well selling magazines that he won a Lionel electric train set and a trip to New York City. On this trip he was chaperoned by the Nolan sisters, his new neighbors on Rosewood.

As an only child, Claiborne was often befriended by hospitable neighbors, and the Nolan sisters, who frequented New York, were foremost in his extended neighborhood family. These kindly matrons took him under their wings, often making him a fourth in their bridge games.

In New York, they introduced the wide-eyed, 13-year-old

Claiborne to the theater, which started a lifelong appreciation for stage shows and an enduring fascination with New York City. Another neighbor, Mr. Garnett Hall, inspired Claiborne to the benefits of Rotary Club, which Claiborne later joined as one of its most dedicated members.

Dr. Margaret Bowen, who lived a few doors down, found Claiborne a job at the High Hampton Inn. In later years, the Nolan sisters helped Claiborne land a job shelving books at the Richmond Public Library. It was a job that got him through his days at the University of Richmond and taught him to use a library. Rosewood became a close-knit community in which Claiborne learned the value of friendship.

The young man's success at salesmanship and the warm support of neighbors helped off-set a plague of early childhood diseases common in those days. "I got 'em all, with the exception of whooping cough," remembered Claiborne. He had measles, diphtheria, scarlet fever and others. Although he was thin and gangly in his youth, Claiborne had a robust constitution and general good health, and as the grandchild of a pharmacist, he was privy to the latest medications.

The neighbors on Rosewood were helpful and friendly, but the neighborhood had another advantage. It was near a school that would leave a lasting impression on Claiborne's life. McQuire's University School was only a few blocks from Claiborne's home on Rosewood, and the education he received there was unusual in that it went well beyond the traditional reading, writing and arithmetic.

Headmaster John Peyton McQuire stressed the fundamentals of learning, but also taught lessons in morality and character-building. It was these lessons that helped fashion a young man into a mature, responsible adult. Mr. McQuire shaped the lives of the boys he taught, many of whom reached important leadership positions as adults.

While they lived with Albert, Martha had enrolled Claiborne

in Ruffners, a public school close to his grandfather's house. It had not been a good experience, however, because students in the school were rough, even by the standards of that era. After only one day in Ruffners, Claiborne wanted to leave.

Martha then enrolled him in Miss Suzie Slaughter's School. "I started school at Miss Suzie Slaughter's, which was a leading private school for younger boys," said Claiborne. "Miss Suzie Slaughter's was within walking distance from my grandfather's home. It was up at Adams and Grace at the time, and it was on the second floor of a building, and there were about 50 students. So many of the young men there went on to McQuire's, like I did."

Miss Suzie Slaughter was an excellent teacher, and Claiborne had a good year there in 1920. Yet after moving to Rosewood, McQuire's was closer.

Claiborne's seven years at McQuire's molded and shaped his character and personality with lasting effect. The school was strong on the work ethic, honor, and generosity. These traits would take precedence for Claiborne and furnish a road map for his morality.

"Going to McQuire's was one of the greatest things that ever happened to me because I had the privilege of being under John Peyton McQuire, who must have been one of the most remarkable men that ever lived in the teaching profession. He had an incredible way with boys, even the worst of the scalawags, and I was fortunate to be thrown in with so many of the people who would later become the top leaders in the city and nation.

"For example, Lewis Powell, who became a Supreme Court Justice, sat just a couple of seats away. I had the privilege of knowing him and others. George Nolde, who headed Nolde Brothers Bakery, was back of me. There were so many fine people in that school.

"Mr. McQuire was a great stickler for the basics. He believed in reading, writing, arithmetic, spelling, and Latin. We took Latin

John Peyton McQuire presents a McQuire's University School diploma to a student in the early 1930s. Photo courtesy of the Virginia Historical Society.

from the day we started McQuire's 'til the day we left, and the same was true for spelling. It was drilled into us. I think it was a very fortunate thing, because I see so many people who can't spell, even after they finish college. Frankly, I don't know how they get through college.

"But about Latin; we had Caesar, Cicero, Virgil, Ovid, and everything there was to be had in Latin. We did not realize it at the time, but we got the basics, not only in English, but in chemistry and foreign languages. We were so very fortunate to have that kind of basic education. In the lower school they believed in giving you ten times the homework you could do just to see what you would do. We'd get home from school at 4:00, then two hours to play, and dinner, and the books.

"The thing that made Mr. McQuire so great was that he had a marvelous knack of instilling the principles of integrity and dedication to duty into the boys. He used to tell a few stories to illustrate his points to the 250 or so boys in the assembly room, and we'd be in tears, even though we had heard that story four times before.

"The number one story that he used to tell, which made such an impression, was about a young man — 14 or 15 — during the War Between the States, who was too young to be in the service, and who was asked by one of the commanders to hold his horse. A stray shell hit him and killed him, but when they found him, he was still holding onto that horse." Here Claiborne paused.

"That still affects me," he said, "but he had that quality. He also had a story about a young man who tried to rescue a young lady who was drowning, and lost his life in the process. But the theme, of course, was that you did what you had to do, no matter what the consequences were. I don't think there could be anyone who ever went to McQuire's who didn't feel the impact of his influence.

"He also had a remarkable capacity to keep order, and that wasn't always easy when you had boys at that age, all 250, in a study room. When someone would throw an orange across the room, he would say, 'All right, gentlemen, who did that?' and the person who did it raised their hand, and he would come to the front of the room, and Mr. McQuire would say, 'My son, why did you do this to me?' You would just as soon go through the floor. That's all he had to say.

"Mr. McQuire was the headmaster and taught some classes himself, but he had five or six other teachers in the school. One was Mr. E. W. Bosworth, who taught Latin. Everybody had Mr. Bosworth, a real stickler. A tough grader, he thought a 'B+' was the highest grade anybody could make. He didn't know an 'A' existed. And if one came in unprepared, Mr. Bosworth would get this faraway look in his eye, and he'd look out of the window to the west and he'd say, 'Gentlemen, it's going to be a lovely evening to watch the sun sinking in the west.'

"He meant that he was going to stay there with them two or three hours after school. And he did it. You soon learned that you'd better prepare, or you'd stay there until 6 or 6:30, depending on how early it got dark. He usually tried to let them out before dark. You learned Latin, I tell you, under Mr. Bosworth."

Claiborne, like many of the future leaders who attended McQuire's, left the school with dedication to duty, to others, and to achieving the best he could. He was shaped by a kind of school that was fast disappearing after the turn of the century. Although the school, founded by the senior McQuire in 1865, lasted until it closed its doors in 1942, the values it taught and the society it served were changing rapidly.

J. Harvie Wilkinson, president of State-Planters Bank, and an alumnus, was quoted in the *Richmond News Leader* in June 1967, saying, "McQuire's was one of the last, great headmaster's schools. Academically, the school was based on a hard core of Latin, English, mathematics and history. But the McQuire's character was a much more important product of the school than any knowledge derived from Virgil or algebra lessons."

Within this exalted and rarefied atmosphere the boys competed for purple, yellow, blue, and white ribbons, each hoping that Mr. McQuire would award him the top-ranking purple ribbon. Claiborne got his share of ribbons, with Martha encouraging every purple one. Yet it was only through hard work and self-discipline that he earned them.

While at McQuire's, one of Claiborne's desires was to make his own spending money. When he saw that the boys at school were always hungry, he asked his grandfather, Albert, to buy 48 Hershey Bars each day. They cost three and a half cents each, and Claiborne sold them to his schoolmates for a dime.

"The way I made an astonishing amount of money was selling Hershey Bars out at the McQuire School. Nobody was doing anything like that. When I left, there were three or four that got the idea after that," chuckled Claiborne. "But when I started I had it all to myself. It was astonishing how many Hershey Bars I could sell a day, and I didn't even have to do anything. The boys would just come by and drop the money on the desk and I'd give them a Hershey Bar, and that was that."

McQuire's demanded commitment and concentration from students, and Claiborne learned those traits well. When he wasn't in school, his magazine and newspaper sales required his time and attention. Life, however, was not all business and academics. On Saturdays in the summertime, Claiborne played first base for the Byrd Park Eagles, a sandlot nine in a league with other area teams, where the competition was fierce.

"I was taller than most of the other kids," said Claiborne, "so I got first base. I was what I would call a fair baseball player; I was adequate, but I enjoyed the sport. After I moved out to Rosewood Avenue we did have the Byrd Park facility there, the baseball diamonds and the tennis courts. So that's when I started playing a little tennis and baseball.

"I was always interested in athletics. When I was 12 to 15 I could have told you every big league ball player, and exactly what his batting average was, and how many hits he had up to that point. You couldn't believe all the stuff that I kept up with in baseball."

Among Claiborne's classmates at McQuire's was Mallory Freeman, with whom Claiborne struck up a lifelong friendship. "Mallory and I have known each other since the beginning of time, just about," said Claiborne. "We have always been close friends."

Mallory was as talented in art as Claiborne was in business. An artist, actor, and painter, Mallory had an exploring and creative mind that he later put to good use at the A. H. Robins Company, where he worked with Claiborne as director of advertising.

G. Mallory Freeman in 1931.

With Mallory Freeman, Claiborne had many memorable boyhood adventures, one of which took place at Willoughby Beach, where Mallory's father had a cabin next to that of his brother, the illustrious author and scholar, Douglas Southall Freeman. Douglas Freeman was the editor of the *Richmond News Leader* and a Pulitzer Prize-winning author whose works included biographies of Robert E. Lee and George Washington. He was a noted authority on the Civil War.

Freeman's daughter, Mary Tyler, was a vivacious girl who joined the boys in their fun on many occasions when Mallory invited Claiborne to visit at the beach.

"Claiborne was a great big, tall, skinny guy with the most beautiful disposition, always smiling and friendly," remembered Mary Tyler Cheek, a leader in Richmond's civic and charitable life. "He would come down to the cottage with Mallory, his best friend, where we had a sailboat, rowboats, canoes, etc. He had no experience with boats, and we teased him by saying that wherever he put his foot, he would turn the boat over."

Mary Tyler Cheek recalls a time when Mallory invited Claiborne to join the Freeman family on a sailing trip up the Chesapeake Bay in a seaworthy boat owned by her father. The boat had a cabin shared by Mallory's and Mary's mothers. Mary Tyler and another cousin, Martha, slept in the cockpit, and Mallory and two other cousins, John and Kingsly, shared the forward deck with Claiborne.

The 12-year-old Claiborne slept fitfully, at best, on the hardwood deck of the pitching sailboat, with only a life preserver as a pillow. "When I awoke in the morning," he said, "I felt like I had been hit by a truck." He was so stiff and sore that it took him some time to loosen up his muscles enough to get up.

"We were gone two days and nights," Claiborne remembered, "and coming back to Willoughby Bay we had the darndest storm you ever saw. The waves got high, water started coming over the side of the boat, and we got the sails down in a hurry. But pretty soon so much water came in that it knocked the engine out completely. So there we were, out there in the middle of the Chesapeake Bay, with no sails and no motor, and I couldn't swim. I was scared to death, and I think everyone else was, too. We had no radio, of course.

"That storm went on for two hours or more, and all of us were bailing water out of the boat, but we survived. We finally got the motor going and got back home, but it was a terrifying experience. As a result, I have never been very crazy about being on a boat. If I'm on a boat, I want it to be the Queen Elizabeth or the QE 2."

The perilous sailboat trip gave rise to a standing joke that has lasted more than 70 years. Mary Tyler Cheek has occasionally commented, with a twinkle in her eyes, that she had known Claiborne since childhood and that they had even slept together. "People would raise their eyebrows and we'd have to explain that sailboat trip," Claiborne explained with a laugh.

Although he didn't like boating, Claiborne very much liked the salt water and the sea air. He joined others in excursions to the beach when he had the time and the money. His church sponsored a trip to Buckroe Beach each year, and beginning with the boarding of the train in Richmond for the day trip, it was a gala day. In the early 1920s Buckroe was a resort with rides, balloons, and festivities for those enjoying the sun, the sand, and the bay.

Claiborne always enjoyed Ocean View and Willoughby. They provided a much needed break from the demands of school and the responsibilities of home. In later summers, when he was detailing his products to doctors in the

RETURN TICKET
——
Second Baptist Church
PICNIC
Friday, June 19, 1931
Buckroe Beach
To
Richmond

Claiborne, at age 23, at the beach with friends in 1933.

Norfolk area, he would get a room along the beach for the night, as it was cooler there. "Along about 7 or 8:00, everything would get very still and very warm," he said. "But an hour or so later, even on the hottest nights, you'd get a wonderful breeze at Willoughby."

Most summers, Martha took her son home to Tennessee for a visit with her family. To reach Rutherford, Tennessee, 100 miles east of Memphis, they took the train from Richmond on a Pullman for overnight travel to Roanoke. There the car was hauled by the Southern Railroad to Bristol, Johnson City, across the lower part of Tennessee, and the northern part of Mississippi, to Corinth, where they changed trains. Then they rode the Mobile and Ohio north to Rutherford, arriving there after two nights and a day.

Rutherford was a sleepy little town where Claiborne had to entertain himself. The postmaster let him go along to the railroad station twice a day to bring back the mailbags. Claiborne enjoyed the great steam engines. They rushed into town, whistles shrieking, with billowing steam mingling with clouds of coal smoke. It made him feel grown-up to shoulder the big canvas mailbags and haul them back to the post office.

When time and weather permitted, Martha drove them 25 miles by horse and buggy over the hills to visit relatives in Milan,

Tennessee. The family enjoyed Martha's musical abilities, and she frequently played for her cousins. It was an enriching month of visiting that renewed Martha's ties with her Taylor relatives, and she always returned to Richmond with new spirit.

Despite the demands of a life that included maintaining her late husband's business, hosting Albert Robins' guests, and caring for her son, Martha never forgot the joys of music. She made a point of instilling this joy in Claiborne by taking him to many performances. Visiting musicians of the highest caliber came to perform at the Academy of Music, Richmond's premier stage production theater at the time. It was located between Eight and Ninth Streets.

"Richmond in those days got many of the better traveling shows," recalled Claiborne. "After they left Broadway they would come through Richmond, and they were well-patronized, or they wouldn't be on the circuit. So I was able to see quite a few of them. Richmond also got all of the top classical artists; violinists like Mischa Elman and Heifitz, and Rachmaninoff and Paderewski, the great pianists and composers."

Many of these great performances were later held at the Mosque, a landmark venue in Richmond that was built in 1930. Claiborne attended most performances.

"My mother being a musician, she drug me literally to all of the concerts. She loved music so, and I went with her whether I wanted to or not. I did have the privilege of hearing all of the top recording artists of the day, whether they be contralto, soprano, tenor, pianist, violinist. You name it, I heard them — Rachmaninoff particularly — two or three times. Rachmaninoff's Prelude in C-sharp Minor ... for some reason that one stuck with me."

Martha's insistence on opening the world of music to Claiborne was one of her greatest gifts to the young man. His appreciation of theater and music enriched his life, just as it had hers. He learned to enjoy classical music, Broadway show tunes, country music and, in later years, the music of the big bands.

However, school was his focal point, and as the end of his senior year neared, Claiborne began to think about where he would go to college. He knew his mother was sacrificing to keep him at McQuire's, and that funds were limited for furthering his education. Then, one day in May 1927, Mr. McQuire called Claiborne into his office.

"Claiborne," he said, "I'm very pleased to tell you that I believe you have the intelligence and the ability to study at the University of Virginia. Therefore, I am awarding you a scholarship so that you may attend the university next fall."

Claiborne was more than flattered. The fact that Mr. McQuire would consider him worthy of attending his alma mater, the University of Virginia, was an honor. "The highest award Mr. McQuire could give was a scholarship to the University of Virginia," said Claiborne.

The scholarship, however, was only $300, and covered only tuition. Room and board would be twice that much. "I got the scholarship and I turned it down because I couldn't afford to go to the University of Virginia," explained Claiborne. "The scholarship only took care of tuition, whereas the main cost in those days was room and board and all the other things that the scholarship didn't take care of."

At the same time Claiborne was offered a $1000 scholarship to the University of Richmond, which helped make up his mind. By attending the University of Richmond, he could ride the streetcar to school, live at home, and cut expenses. Reluctantly, he told Mr. McQuire of his decision, and enrolled at the University of Richmond in September 1927.

Claiborne's departure from McQuire's was a turning point. It was there he had learned the value of dedication to his studies through the expectations of the headmaster and teachers. He had also come to embrace the virtues of honesty and integrity espoused by Mr. McQuire. Those lessons, both practical and character-building, served him throughout his adult life.

THE UNIVERSITY OF RICHMOND
RICHMOND, VIRGINIA
F. W. BOATWRIGHT, PRESIDENT
S. WEST TABB, VICE-PRESIDENT AND TREASURER

THE UNIVERSITY
INCLUDES
RICHMOND COLLEGE
W. L. PRINCE, DEAN
THE T. C. WILLIAMS SCHOOL OF LAW
J. H. BARNETT, JR., SECRETARY
WESTHAMPTON COLLEGE
MAY L. KELLER, DEAN

SUMMER SCHOOL
W. L. PRINCE, DIRECTOR

P. O. UNIVERSITY OF RICHMOND, VA.

July 7, 1930.

Mr. E. Claiborne Robins,

    2412 Rosewood Avenue,

        Richmond, Va.

Dear Sir:

    I am authorized by our trustees to
grant you a minor scholarship in Richmond College
for the session 1930-31, based on the $1,000
scholarship founded by Mr. James D. Crump.
Please let me know promptly if you accept this
scholarship and will matriculate in September.
We shall be glad to have you continue your work
in the University of Richmond for a degree.

                Sincerely yours,

                F. W. Boatwright
                            President.

University of Richmond President Frederick W. Boatwright grants Claiborne a scholarship in 1930.

"It's interesting how one thing leads to another in your life," reflected Claiborne. "I've often said you go down the path of life and you don't know why, but you may take a slight left turn and you meet somebody who changes your whole life. And if you hadn't made that left turn you'd have gone straight ahead, or made a right, and you never would have met them."

Mr. John Peyton McQuire was waiting for Claiborne at a crucial juncture. As a tribute to that chance meeting, Claiborne had carried on the ideals of his most noted mentor. A teacher and father figure, Mr. McQuire furnished moral guidance for Claiborne. This, coupled with the enduring drive of his mother and the values she extolled through sacrifice, channeled young Claiborne down a clear path.

As a result, his foundation was built of solid stuff that would endure the weight of major responsibilities and pivotal decisions. The influences of his mother and Mr. McQuire provided the moral underpinnings for a young man destined for great accomplishments and the trials that would come with them.

Claiborne's philosophical roots can be traced to the people he most respected. One of the essential expressions of his philosophy is personal effort and industry, which he learned from his mother and from Mr. McQuire, and which he would later teach to his family and company employees.

"If you could instill in your children — and I worry about this for my grandchildren, because, fortunately, or unfortunately, they don't have to work — but if you could just get a little of this in everybody, it would be tremendous. I don't know anything that you could pass onto your children more important than values like integrity, loyalty, dedication and generosity."

III

THE STUDENT

It took Claiborne an hour to travel from his home on Rosewood Avenue, near Byrd Park, to the college campus in the far west end of Richmond. First he caught the streetcar that came up Robinson Street to Broad Street station, then he changed cars and went out the Grove Avenue line to the entrance of the college.

During his trips to and from the campus, Claiborne spent most of his time doing homework or catching up on the required reading. The streetcar ride cost a nickel, and it was a routine he would follow from 1927 until 1931.

The University of Richmond in 1928 was quite different from the nationally ranked, private university that it would become under Claiborne's beneficiary role in later years. The lake that divided the campus, and the educational policy of the time, adequately separated the men and women of the institution.

Richmond College for men and Westhampton College for women provided separate campuses and living, dining, and studying facilities for their students. The school was also considerably smaller than it is today.

On the men's side of the campus, the only buildings in 1927 were Boatwright Library, Millhiser Gymnasium, the Refectory, Thomas and Jeter Halls, the Science Quadrangle, and Ryland Hall. Westhampton College, the women's side, was comprised of North Court residence hall and Keller Hall.

In keeping with the moral principles of the times the sexes were carefully segregated. Men and women could meet for joint university convocations only at Cannon Memorial Chapel. There were also dances given by the social committees of each college, and men and women could participate together in honor societies, debating clubs, fraternities and other clubs.

The University of Richmond had become a university only seven years before Claiborne enrolled in 1927, although its history reached back nearly a century. The men's division, Richmond College, had been founded in 1832. The institution had moved to its present location in the west end of Richmond in 1914.

Dr. Frederic W. Boatwright, who was to remain president of the institution for 50 years, led the move to the west Richmond location. The college was well established, but there was a constant struggle for operating funds, and there was no endowment fund for the promise of future growth. There were, however, men and women on the faculty who were master teachers and whose reputation for scholarship was unquestioned.

Claiborne joined other freshman in the first year liberal arts classes of English, history, math and science, since he had no idea that he would go into the family business. Like many freshmen, he was uncertain of his future and thought it best to take a general course of study.

Although Claiborne enjoyed his classes and worked hard, he had no particular favorites on the college faculty. He remembered one psychology professor, however, Dr. Robert C. Astrop, who was such a great lecturer that "he could hold a class spellbound day after day." Claiborne took four years of psychology and felt that those classes were quite useful to him during his career in dealing with employees, salesmen and customers.

Another popular professor was Dr. Samuel Chiles Mitchell, a history teacher who inspired many students. Claiborne recalled, "I think he gave me the only 'C' I got at the university, but Mitchell was interesting in that he kind of opened your eyes to things. At the beginning of the semester he would pick out some student and ask a question such as: 'Mr. Smith, you go to New York City, get off the train, and what is the next thing you do?'

"Woe be to the student if he did not know the answer: 'You head for the Metropolitan Museum of Art.' The reason, according to Dr. Mitchell, was that there is more education to be obtained if you spend days there than you could get spending the same time elsewhere."

Claiborne's years at the University of Richmond were devoted to getting good grades and earning money to help get himself through school. While classmates were joining fraternities and other campus clubs, Claiborne spent his time studying and working.

On one occasion, however, he laid down his books and joined in his favorite summer sport. "One of my fondest memories was the only time I participated in a sport at the University of Richmond," said Claiborne. "They had a student game with the U of R baseball team. It was just an exhibition game, which they had some of the students play in. I was playing first base, and the highest compliment ever paid me was by Mack Pitt, who was coaching the baseball team. He saw me playing first base and said, 'Where has that fellow been? Why didn't he come out for the team?'"

Claiborne, despite his intense love for baseball, focused his energies on education and working his way through school. "I've always followed baseball, basketball, and football," he affirmed. "They are my three favorites and I love them all. I'm a Redskins fan along with so many Richmonders. I just didn't have the time," he recalled, "working at the library to help get through."

One of Claiborne's neighbors, Miss Nolan, had helped him get a job at the Richmond Public Library. Claiborne worked after school hours and stacked books until 9 p.m. As he became more familiar with the library he helped out in the reference department, directing patrons to the proper books. In addition to the 25 cents an hour pay, he learned how to use a library, an asset he put to good use in his academic career.

The money he earned from the library job, added to the $1,000 scholarship from American National Bank, helped get Claiborne through his first year, and he did well enough that the bank notified him that he would have the scholarship for his sophomore year.

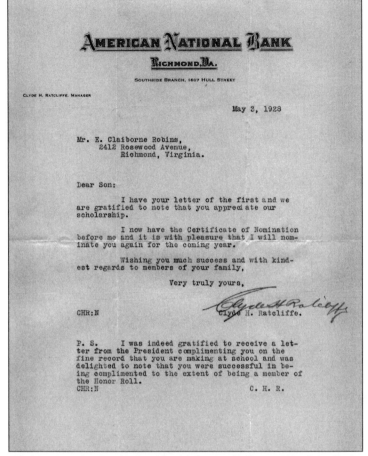

The letter from American National Bank informing Claiborne of his scholarship for 1928-29.

When he finished his second year at the university on the dean's list, Claiborne knew exactly what he wanted to do with his summer. He had loved his visit to New York City with the Nolan sisters when he won the magazine contest at age 13. The excitement of the city and the dazzling Broadway shows left him filled with a desire to enjoy more of the big city's charms.

"Mother," he said in May 1929, "I'd like to get a summer job in New York." Martha was horrified by the announcement. She knew how much Claiborne loved the city, but was reluctant to let this shy young man go off on his own. He had not lived away from home by himself, there were lots of temptations in New York, and he had no job there. How could she let her young and innocent son face all the potential perils of a huge city where he knew no one?

Martha, however, knew her son well and saw how the lessons of character he had learned at McQuire's had shaped his life and personality. Her trust in Claiborne prevailed, and she let him go, though no doubt many of her friends and neighbors questioned her decision.

"She was horrified," Claiborne remembered, "and so were our neighbors and friends. 'You're not going to let him go to New York by himself, at 18 years of age, the wicked city?' But fortunately, I didn't have any money and so you don't get into much trouble if you don't have any money. It's amazing how that's a moral influence," he laughed. "It usually costs money to sin."

That June Claiborne caught the train for New York and began the first real adventure of his life. He wouldn't fully realize until later what incredible luck he had making his own way. On his second day there he walked into the Hub Employment Agency, which he described as "a ratty-looking place on Sixth Ave." The room was filled with men, most shabbily dressed, sitting on benches, smoking, reading, and waiting for a job.

Claiborne, with a coat and tie, was the best-dressed man there. A man at a desk in the front of the room looked up, saw Claiborne and beckoned to him. The man asked him what he wanted to do. Claiborne told him he was looking for summer employment, to which the man nodded and scribbled down an address.

That address would lead Claiborne to The Upjohn Company, where they needed a mail clerk. It was sheer luck, or an angel on his shoulder guiding him, as Claiborne strongly believes, that out of thousands of businesses in New York, he had been sent to a pharmaceutical company.

After a brief interview, Claiborne got the job and reported to Mr. W. E. Broadbent. The future CEO of one of Upjohn's future competitors, the A. H. Robins Company, would be working as a clerk in the mail room.

"The miracle of that story is getting a job the next day after I got up there, and getting it with a pharmaceutical company, The Upjohn Company," mused Claiborne. "I always felt the good Lord must have had a hand in that because the odds of that happening must have been one out of millions."

Newly employed, Claiborne went back to the agency and paid $6 for the job placement. Though it was over 60 years later that he recounted the story, Claiborne's memory for names was still as clear as when he worked at Upjohn, and he fondly recalled his co-workers.

The receipt Claiborne received from the Hub Employment Agency for placing him at The Upjohn Company in June 1929.

Burt Thornton, a brusque New Yorker, worked with him in the mail room, and Claiborne learned much about New York from him. Apparently, Thornton was very interested in women, and he often remarked on the charms of those who visited the mail room. Claiborne's mind, at that point, was more occupied with learning his new job and discovering the attractions of the country's largest city. He gave little thought to finding a girl friend. "I worked all day and didn't have enough money to date anyway," he said. "I was busy working and trying to make something out of my life."

THE STUDENT

Now that he had a job, which started at $20 a week, but increased to $22 within three weeks, the 18-year-old needed a place to live. His needs were more than met at the Redfern House, at 23 West 76th Street, near Central Park, which he described as "kind of a fancy boarding house, like you see in plays. How in the world the rates were as low as they were, I don't know. There were individual tables, with servants in tuxedos. You got breakfast and dinner and a room for $18 a week.

"I had a good breakfast and kind of saved up for dinner. The food was not gourmet, but it was all right and plenty of it. My lunch was the same thing every day, peanut butter crackers and a Coke. That cost a dime. My one splurge for  lunch was when there was a matinee performance at a Times Square theater on Saturday. I'd take the subway to Times Square and go to the Automat, which in those days was a great thing for people who didn't have a lot of money. They had a beef pie for 25 cents. You had a whole meal if you had that. Then I'd get a slice of apple or peach pie for ten cents. I looked forward very fondly to having the beef pie on those occasions," he said.

Claiborne wrote his mother in Richmond, telling her of his job and the boarding house address. "Don't worry," he told her, "I'm doing just fine." Martha wrote him back, informing him that he had made the dean's list at the university and that she would send him clothes soon. She was proud of her son for his accomplishment at school, and now for his independence in the city.

For Claiborne, the city held enchantment. He loved New York. "It has a pulse you can almost feel. Some people hate it, but it has a certain excitement about it, and for cultural advantages, you can't beat it."

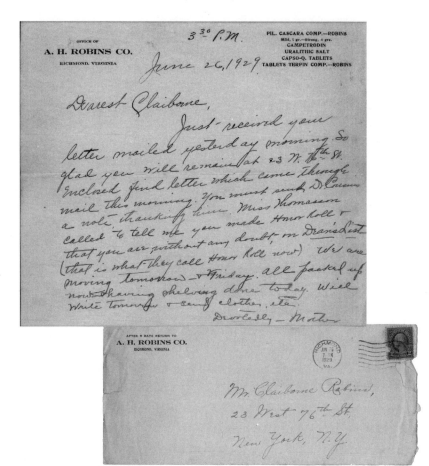

The letter Martha wrote to Claiborne in June 1929.

He was enthralled by the theater and saw hit shows from "the dollar seats up in the roost" or the $1 standing room behind the orchestra. Those summer performances fed his continuing fascination for the theater, a lifelong joy. "Once, in later years, I went to New York and saw six shows in a week," he said, "but it was a great mistake. You couldn't remember what you had seen at the end of the week."

In that wonderful summer of 1929, mesmerized by the magic of the theater, Claiborne thrilled to performances of Ed Wynne in "Simple Simon" and Cole Porter's "Fifty Million Frenchmen."

Other hits that year were "From Morn to Midnight," "The Brothers Karamazov," "Strange Interlude," "Heartbreak House," and "Hit the Deck." Claiborne saw as many as he could. He wandered about the city as New Yorkers were humming the newest popular tunes, "You're the Cream in My Coffee," and "Button Up Your Overcoat."

The latest songs by Jerome Kern, Richard Rogers, George and Ira Gershwin, and Irving Berlin could be heard as he walked past the doors of the bustling bars and restaurants. Bookstore windows featured stacks of the latest novels, including Ernest Hemingway's "A Farewell to Arms," and "All Quiet on the Western Front," by Erich Maria Remarque. Claiborne, however, had no time for reading. He worked until 5 p.m., rode the subway home by 6 p.m., ate dinner, and relaxed in the evenings by listening to the radio and perusing the newspapers. Although he lived a few blocks from Central Park, he never made the time to visit one of New York's greatest attractions.

On alternate Saturdays, when he wasn't at the theater, he went to the great baseball stadiums of the day: Yankee Stadium and the Polo Grounds, home of John McGraw and the New York Giants. Claiborne loved baseball and saw the diamond heroes of the day. He played baseball all through school and was an enthusiastic and skilled player. This same youngster would one day live out the dream of owning a minor league baseball club and entertaining the infamous Yankee manager Casey Stengel.

As a youngster, professional baseball was all magic and romance, and from his seat in the bleachers he cheered the booming home runs by Yankee great Babe Ruth, and joined the crowd in chanting "Poosh 'em Up!" when Yankee second baseman Tommy Lazzeri came to bat. Lazzeri was a favorite of the Yankee fans in the summer of 1929, and they urged him to hit the ball into the seats. Claiborne yelled himself hoarse at the play of future baseball Hall of Fame players Bill Dickey and Lou Gehrig of the Yankees. "It was just a wonderful opportunity to see some of the great baseball stars," he said.

Entertainment was confined mostly to weekends, however, so for the rest of the week Claiborne was frugal, hard-working, and responsible. He flourished during his first fling with independence. For a young man imbued with the bright lights of the big city, Claiborne showed he was capable of taking care of himself while partaking in the cultural mecca that was New York.

"The thing I'm most proud of is that I didn't have to write home for money," Claiborne said. He earned enough at Upjohn to indulge his love of the theater and baseball, and he was well liked at the firm. The job also gave him an opportunity to see what a pharmaceutical company was like. At the time, Upjohn was one of the largest pharmaceutical companies in the country.

"I could see what the potential was," Claiborne acknowledged. His job included making the deposits of the day's receipts in First National City Bank, about three blocks away. He was always impressed by the amount of the deposits, which sometimes were as much as $25,000. "After all, I was coming from Robins, where we probably deposited $25,000 in a year."

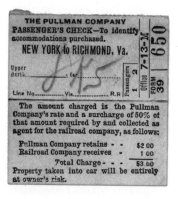

Claiborne worked efficiently and faithfully at Upjohn, and everyone liked "Eddie" that summer of 1929. He returned to Richmond in September to enroll at the University of Richmond for his junior year, and again he ranked near the top of his class. His co-worker, Burt Thornton, wrote him in December to wish him a merry Christmas.

Although he had shown little interest in girls, despite Burt's enticements, an introduction by his neighbor, changed that. Dr. Margaret Bowen invited him to meet her niece, Mary Crockett, who was visiting from Tazewell, Virginia. "Crock" was a pretty brown-haired girl with a quick smile, and she was Claiborne's first date.

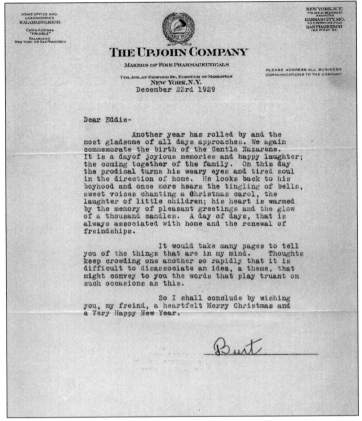

Claiborne's friend, Burt Thornton, at The Upjohn Company sends "Eddie" season's greetings in December 1929.

Before he met Crock, Claiborne's attention had been concentrated on getting an education and earning money to help his mother. Now the girl with the chestnut hair had that special something that attracted him. There was more than a spark of interest between Crock and the lanky, shy collegian, and this mutual interest led Claiborne to make a couple of visits to Tazewell.

It was not easy to travel to Tazewell in 1930. At the wheel of his mother's Model A Ford, Claiborne drove from Richmond to Roanoke, up the mountain to Christiansburg, and on to Bluefield, West Virginia, before crossing back over the state line to get to

Tazewell. It was a trip of more than 300 miles that required seven or eight hours in the car.

Crock was a student at Queens College in Raleigh, North Carolina, and Claiborne and his friend Mallory once made a trip to see her there. Mallory had no arrangements for a date at Queens, but was glad to go along with Claiborne for the ride. The two buddies took off for the weekend, laughing and joking as they rolled down the highway to Charlotte.

There was one small problem: Queens students were not allowed out with anyone except family. "I think she signed out with me as her brother," Claiborne recalled with a chuckle. Crock stayed in his mind and life for quite a while, but the distance to Tazewell eventually cooled his interest, and other girls were beginning to catch his eye.

Dr. Bowen did another nice thing for Claiborne that had a lasting effect on his life. Her nephew was the manager of the High Hampton Inn, a popular resort in the mountains of North Carolina, and she recommended Claiborne to him for summer employment as a bellhop. The job paid little, but the tips were generous, and Claiborne worked at the resort during the summers after his freshman and junior years.

Travel being a more significant obstacle than it is today, the trip by train from Richmond to Cashiers, North Carolina, in 1928 was long by most standards. The fashionable resort was located at the western tip of North Carolina, closer to Georgia, Tennessee and South Carolina than to Richmond.

On his first visit, a mix-up in communications occurred and Claiborne was not expected when he arrived at the train depot across the mountain from High Hampton. When he called the inn, he was told to find local transportation. The depot manager called a local man who agreed to drive him. On the way over the mountain, the driver spied a rabbit alongside the road, and without telling Claiborne, he got out of the truck, grabbed his shotgun and fired. The deafening boom caught Claiborne off

48

guard and gave the tired young traveler quite a start.

Tucked away in the mountains, the High Hampton Inn was a favorite of vacationers from all over the South. It was built early in the 19th century by Wade Hampton II as a summer refuge. The 3,600-foot elevation provided cool temperatures and relief from the lowland heat and humidity.

Hampton built a hunting lodge, smokehouses, barns, and slave quarters, and the refuge was inherited by Wade Hampton III, who became a Confederate general, a governor of South Carolina, and a U.S. senator. In later years, 19 cottages were built and furnished with simple pine furniture. Most had porches where customers could rest in rocking chairs facing the lake or mountains.

Claiborne's post was on the front steps of the inn to welcome guests, many of whom had been coming there for decades. His job was to help them get settled and carry their bags to their rooms. Recreation at the inn was mainly relaxation, though tennis courts and a golf course were available. There was no swimming pool, but a magnificent lake was a short distance away for those who could tolerate the cold water.

Guests working up an appetite could count on satisfying their hunger in the dining room, which served delicious dishes of the time: sausage bread, cranberry Waldorf salad, fried chicken, peanut soup, peach ice cream, and plum duff — a pudding of prunes, flour, and eggs. Claiborne feasted on the good food with an appetite sharpened by hard work and the brisk mountain air.

In the middle of the week, when the departures and arrivals were slower, he had a chance to relax a bit, and learned to play golf on the excellent course at the inn. Having learned to play bridge with the Nolan sisters, he was often invited to play with the guests. At the end of the summers he returned to Richmond with money in his pocket, and was always eager to return to school.

Claiborne had been concerned about his grandfather for some time, as Albert insisted on keeping the apothecary open in spite of his failing health. He did what he could in his spare time to help Albert, but it became clear in 1929 that the old gentleman could not keep going.

Urged by his family, Albert closed the apothecary and retired. Bedridden, but alert, he died six years later in 1935 at age 92. As the namesake of the A. H. Robins Company, Albert Hartley Robins left Claiborne the sole male heir. His death closed an eventful chapter of the Robins family story and of Richmond history.

Claiborne continued concentrating on his studies, and he did what he could to help the family finances. The Great Depression interceded, however, and in the fall of his junior year the stock market tumbled. It was as much the talk of the campus as anywhere else. Uncertainty was rampant, and many students wondered if they would be able to return to the university after the term.

Martha stretched the family budget a little more to assure that her son could finish his studies. The grim economic conditions hindered drug sales and hammered down even further the net income of the A. H. Robins Company, whose main products at the time were Campetrodin, a lineament, Uralythic salt for arthritis, and the tried and true Cascara.

Claiborne worked hard during the summers because he was aware of the burden his mother was under during his college years. Funding his education during the Depression became a trial for her, and the struggles she endured elevated Martha in her son's eyes. School became a great gift for which Claiborne has been forever grateful.

"My mother made great sacrifices to put me through school," recalled Claiborne. "She did not have a great deal. She did have her own home on Rosewood Avenue and we lived comfortably. I don't mean we were suffering, but she didn't have anything to spare and, of course, she had that terrible disaster. Some of the officers of American National Bank had persuaded her to buy preferred stock at American National, and when they went under in the '30s the preferred stock was worthless.

THE STUDENT

"The common stock was wiped out, the preferred stock was wiped out, so she lost the income from the preferred stock, and what little savings she had was mostly in that. So all she had was the small business, which had dwindled down to about a little less than $5,000 a year. I think she was drawing $10 a week out of that business. She had very little income. I think she borrowed a little on the house — she did own that. Due to her sacrifice, which I was well aware of, I suppose that inspired me."

As Richmond teetered on the brink of the Depression, the 22-story Central National Bank, Richmond's tallest skyscraper at the time, had been completed on Third and Broad Streets, where Claiborne had sold newspapers as a boy. Headed by William H. Schwartzschild, the new building was a heavy financial burden as the economy faltered. Yet the bank's excellent leadership guided the firm through the lean years, and it ultimately prospered. In later years, Central National Bank became one of A. H. Robins' strongest financial partners.

During his senior year, at a time when he especially needed the extra cash, Claiborne put to practical use his considerable skills in language. He was an outstanding scholar in both French and German. When two Medical College of Virginia professors needed tutoring in German in order to read German scientific journals, Claiborne was recommended by his language professor, Dr. Woodford Hackley.

"I minored in German, why, I don't know, but I was excellent at German," said Claiborne. "I was proficient enough that my professor recommended me to these professors down at MCV. One of them was Dr. Harvey Haig, who was head of the department of Pharmacology. He had a lot of scientific papers that he wanted translated, and he also wanted to be tutored so he could read German. I tutored him for two years and they paid me very well. Today I've forgotten everything that I ever knew about German except for an expression my dear mother used to have, 'Habe geduld mein lieber Kind,' 'Have patience, my dear child,'

I think it is." Claiborne said today that he remembers only enough French to get by in a French restaurant.

Professor Harvey Haig and two associates paid Claiborne $6,000 over three years for his instruction. "Imagine my nerve at coaching a professor," said Claiborne. "Six thousand dollars in those days was a lot of money, but as you can see, one reason why I never got into trouble, I reckon, when I was young, is that I didn't have time. I was always working at something." Claiborne's earnings were a great help in financing his education at the university and later, at the School of Pharmacy.

Martha made another sacrifice halfway through Claiborne's last year at the university. She gave him a new Model A Ford as a graduation present. Claiborne contributed some of his income, and with money his mother had somehow squirreled away, he became the proud owner of a $500 car that enabled him to get back and forth from school and his job with much greater ease.

"I think only three students had cars there, although several of the faculty kept them on the campus," Claiborne recalled.

Claiborne still did not know what he was going to do with his life, but toward the end of his senior year at the University of

Richmond, he began to think seriously about the family business. He knew all too well of his mother's struggle to keep the company going and how the business had dwindled to a dangerous level.

The gross sales of $25,000 achieved in the last year of his father's life had shrunk to a low of $4,800 by the time Claiborne graduated in 1931. He was only 20, one of the youngest graduates of the school, and his friends from The Upjohn Company sent him a letter of congratulations for graduating with

Claiborne's University of Richmond graduation portrait taken in 1931.

honors. Claiborne had reached a crucial point in his life, the choosing of a career.

, That summer, Claiborne made his decision. His mother's long, hard battle to save the A. H. Robins Company helped make up his mind. "She had struggled so hard and so long to hold the company together. It wasn't very much, but it was still there and it had a good name. I felt that I would be letting her down if I didn't come into the company."

Claiborne realized, however, that he needed a pharmacy degree if he was to lead the A. H. Robins Company. He had earned a degree in English Literature with minors in French and German, but his courses at the University of Richmond had not included chemistry, the heart of pharmacy.

He applied to the pharmacy school of the Medical College of Virginia, and was admitted in September of 1931. The curriculum in the pharmacy division of MCV had been extended from two to three years in 1926, and enrollment requirements had been tightened under the leadership of Dean Wortley F. Rudd.

"I had made the mistake of not taking any chemistries at Richmond, and when I decided to go into pharmacy, I needed four chemistries. I had everything I needed to complete pharmacy in two years except for those chemistries, so I took two chemistries my first year. I was taking organic before first year chemistry."

The institution had made significant progress under the leadership of a new president, Dr. William T. Sanger, who set out to raise $1 million to build a new dormitory, laboratory and outpatient building. The stature of the college had grown, and its graduates had good reputations.

Claiborne plunged into the classwork immediately. "I had two labs at the same time," he said, "and I had to keep running from one floor to the next when we had to do experiments. I'd ask the person next to me in each course to keep the lab from blowing up. I had a tough road on that. I took one course in chemistry in summer school." By bearing down, he kept his grades at a respectable level. "I think my professors may have had compassion for me," he said.

Claiborne had little time to participate in student life at MCV, but he was elected Athletic Council Representative for the freshman pharmacy class. He was invited to join Kappa Psi fraternity, and still worked hard enough to make the pharmacy school dean's list. In his senior year, he was chosen secretary of the Mortar & Pestle Club, an honor society.

"I don't know how I did it," he said of his achievement, but he felt an urgency to succeed at school and he pushed himself hard, finishing the three-year course in two years. Claiborne didn't earn a medal for achieving the best grades in his class, as his father had at MCV in 1896, but he was near the top in all his courses.

At graduation, MCV gave Claiborne a degree in pharmacy, but he still had to pass the State Board of Pharmacy test in order to practice, a task that forced him to study with grim determination. The test was both written and practical, and the practical was so comprehensive that it required students to manufacture suppositories.

Claiborne explained that the suppositories were made from glycerin, which had to be worked at low temperature. In the non-air conditioned classroom, this required 50 pounds of ice in a sink, and students froze their hands during the practical. Cold hands were good for about three minutes, Claiborne said, who managed to sail through the test.

"I didn't do anything for three weeks before I took my boards," said Claiborne. "I cornered myself in my room and I didn't go out. As soon as I had breakfast I was studying and had lunch and went right back to studying and then, after dinner, I went right back to studying, at least until midnight. But I tell you, when I took that state board, I don't mind saying so, I didn't miss anything."

With his educational training complete, Claiborne found a job at Van Pelt & Brown, a Richmond apothecary. He worked there a brief time before coming to work for the family company, where his mother had held the reins since his father's death 20 years before.

Claiborne bore the confidence of youth and, despite the Depression, he embraced the promise of the future. It felt right for him to employ the natural salesmanship he had practiced most of his life and to apply himself to the business the way he had applied himself to school.

His future was now with the A. H. Robins Company and the pharmaceutical industry. The time had come for Claiborne to put his well-rounded education, both formal and informal, to the practical test.

IV

THE DETAILMAN

In January 1933 Martha Taylor Robins had gone over the A. H. Robins Company annual report carefully. She knew every figure well, and the news was not good. Gross sales were down, net profits were down, and expenses kept creeping up. Having relied solely on her own resources, she now hoped that Claiborne could help keep the company going when he graduated from the Medical College of Virginia in June.

For 21 years, since Claiborne was two, Martha had held the company together as its director. She occasionally hired employees for sales and shipments of medications, but few had produced much revenue. The Depression had hurt the company, and gross sales had dropped from $25,000 in 1912 to $4,800 in 1933. It was during this slump that Claiborne, fresh out of college, joined the firm.

The little company was in desperate need of promotion and new leadership. Martha and her lone employee, Alma May Robertson, handled sales and correspondence. They labored in basement quarters at Sixth and Main Streets, where the rent was $20 a month. The address, 5 South Sixth Street, was the second location for the company, as Martha had been forced to move to cheaper rents in an effort to hold operational costs to a minimum.

There they repackaged and shipped to wholesalers the drugs that Martha bought and labeled with the Robins name. Martha's helper, Alma, or "Miss Teeny," as she was known because of her small size, remained with the company for more than 40 years and became the firm's first employee to retire in 1949.

"Her loyalty and dedication and willingness to work at a small salary helped the company to survive," Claiborne recalled. "The fact that she practically worked for nothing didn't bother her."

It took courage for Claiborne to enter the business world

during the Depression when the outlook was so grim. Federal agencies had been established to help the jobless in 1933, including the labor force of 11,000 then out of work in Richmond. President Franklin D. Roosevelt, in an effort to avert a national financial crisis, closed the doors of the nation's banks for four days in March of that year.

One of those banks was American Bank and Trust in Richmond, which was closed permanently. Its stockholders, including Martha Robins, completely lost their investments. The $10,000 she had invested there was a significant part of her resources. Her remaining asset was the A. H. Robins Company, and she drew a meager $10 a week salary from the firm. She had to borrow money on her Rosewood Avenue home to get Claiborne through school.

When Claiborne reported for work in 1933 the company was in debt. The A. H. Robins Company had introduced no new products in the 20-year period since his father's death, relying primarily on their two principal products, Robins Cascara Compounds, mild and strong. Three other products, Uralythic Salt, Herotone Tablets, and Capso-quinine Tablets, were barely moving.

Martha had tried to promote the products and, from time to time, had hired detailmen. Unfortunately, they cost the company more in pay than they produced in orders. She also tried some direct mail and some limited sampling of the products, but with little success. She had neither the funds nor the expertise to be very effective. Meanwhile, newer drugs sold by aggressive salesmen representing competing pharmaceutical companies were taking over the market.

With college behind him, and having passed the state examination board without error, Claiborne was armed with equal amounts of youthful confidence and self discipline. "It never occurred to me that I could fail," he said of those uncertain days, and his first act was securing a $2,000 loan from Central National Bank. This allowed him to set out on the road to boost the company sales.

"We were already customers of the bank, and our account was very small, yet we got the loan without collateral," Claiborne said. That transaction was fortuitous for both parties. Claiborne got the funds to build his company and, in return, the bank gained a very loyal customer. The millions of dollars later earned by the A. H. Robins Company provided Central National many profits.

In the summer of 1933 Claiborne tossed his suitcase into his Model A Ford and headed for Washington, D.C., where he began to promote Robins Cascara. It still had a good reputation with physicians, especially the older physicians, some of whom remembered his father. Some of the younger doctors also remembered Robins Cascara, but there were many younger doctors who had not heard of A. H. Robins. They listened attentively as Claiborne pitched his wares in his gracious, sincere manner, but it wasn't long before he began to realize that the company was not going to prosper on Cascara alone.

After two months in Washington he returned to Richmond, his mind occupied much of the time with developing new products for the company. He studied medical journals for ideas, and one particular article caught his eye. It described the advantages of using belladonna alkaloids together with phenobarbital.

From that article Claiborne put together a new product that started the A. H. Robins Company on its way to a billion dollar concern. The new product was Donnatal, a compound that physicians could prescribe for a number of medical conditions. Claiborne used the magazine article that had stimulated the idea as a means of promoting the product in sales meetings.

The new drug was highly successful, becoming the mainstay of the Robins inventory. It is still on the market over 60 years later. "A doctor could use it for probably one in every five patients he sees," Claiborne explained, "and doctors knew the value of the ingredients."

The new drug was the first of many the young salesman created, often while sitting in doctor's offices thinking about products that could help the suffering of the ill during the 1930s. He concentrated on those products that could make everyday life easier, using tried and true drugs, much as his grandfather Albert had in his time.

The belladonna in Donnatal had been used by Europeans for centuries. Other products he would create would use kaolin, an ancient Egyptian product, and codeine, a drug once used by the Babylonians.

Claiborne enjoyed selling, and it came easily to him. His approach to selling was to know his products, explain them to the physicians, and let the products speak for themselves, a practice called "detailing."

As physicians came to know the reliability of his goods they became open to the new products he offered. Claiborne concentrated on Donnatal in those early years, using his one advantage over competing companies: Donnatal was his primary product.

"I don't think other companies realized what a market there was for Donnatal," remarked Claiborne, "and the other products on the market at the time did not have the volume of sales that would indicate a potential $10 million product."

Even with the new product, progress was slow. Gross sales only increased gradually. In 1934 the company lost $500, but the next year it was in the black with a $100 profit. In addition to Cascara and Donnatal, the company had a theobromine and phenobarbital product, a compound called Theorate. It also had an iron product, Bironex. Robins continued to use Smith, Kline, and Merck, Sharp and Dohme to manufacture its drugs because the A. H. Robins Company had no laboratory facilities of its own.

Claiborne's days on the road were long but interesting, and when he came back to Richmond he was heavily involved in the administrative duties of the company. There was little time to play, but Claiborne occasionally joined his Richmond peers in sports, theater and other activities.

He was active in the Second Baptist Church, which his

grandfather had helped establish before the turn of the century. The church had a softball team, and Claiborne played as often as he could. He also enjoyed the church bowling team. A newspaper account of that period recorded his achievement of bowling a remarkable 330 set, only four pins under the league record. He was the high scoring bowler for Second Baptist.

It was while he was bowling that he met Marguerite Henley, a brown-haired girl who became his companion for the next several years. She was attractive and worked as secretary to an executive of the Life Insurance Company of Virginia. The couple enjoyed tennis, bowling, and the local restaurants. They shared a strong interest in the theater and were often in the audience at the Empire or Bijou theaters for the latest movies, or at the Academy for a Broadway show. Their romance flourished, and they might have married had it not been for a sales trip to Waco, Texas in 1937.

Claiborne with Marguerite Henley in the mid-1930s.

Claiborne was a superb salesman. He was sincere, he knew pharmacology, and he represented his products well. His wide grin and his gentle manner made him believable and trustworthy. The shyness that had characterized his early years was gradually replaced by a confidence built on the growing faith in his products.

"I have been told that I have been successful because I come across as being very sincere," he said. "I had no sales training, but I did two things: I worked hard and I saw more doctors per day than the average man."

A smile, said Claiborne, often pays dividends far into the future. "I think youngsters should know the importance of a smile and know the importance of letting people know that you are glad to see them. These are all very intangible things, but they are important."

A pleasant disposition coupled with untiring effort were Claiborne's hallmarks, and they created a good rapport with the doctors to whom he detailed A. H. Robins medications. Claiborne drove hard to boost the sales of his company.

"What I would do is go to 12 drug stores right off the bat. I would leave them a sample of what we were going to be detailing the doctors with so that if they got a prescription they wouldn't say, 'Well, we don't have this.' They already had a small quantity.

"What they'd say, then, was 'Well, I just have a few tablets, but I'll order the rest of this prescription for you.' I would do that first and then I'd get each pharmacy to give me a dozen — usually they were willing to do it — of who the largest prescribers in the city were. When you get a list from 12 different stores, you frequently find some of the same names, of course. But others would have new names, so I was able to get a pretty good gauge.

"I could always get about 150 top-notch prescribers from the druggists. Then I would try to find out something about each one. I'd ask the pharmacist if any of these names he'd given me were specialists, such as OB/GYN or surgeons, or whether they were internal medicine or general practice, or so forth, so that I would know when I went in to see the doctor I wouldn't go in and be talking to an OB/GYN about something in neurology."

If he was going to be in a city for more than a week, Claiborne would find a boarding house. It was cheaper than a motel and he was intent on keeping costs down. "It had the advantage of furnishing you two meals, which you wouldn't get in a motel or bed and breakfast," he said.

Claiborne traveled south and west, from North Carolina to

Texas, and found a ready reception by doctors. He covered Texas, Kansas, Missouri, Oklahoma, Kentucky, Tennessee, Virginia, the District of Columbia, North Carolina and South Carolina.

Demographics also expanded the company's business as patients using A. H. Robins medications sometimes moved, and when they moved, they asked for Robins products. A. H. Robins Company was eventually doing business from New York and Boston across the country to Denver, though no one from the company actually called on doctors in much of that area.

Some states were more productive than others, but Virginia was not one of them. Although Claiborne worked his native state, he spent more time in more receptive markets. He thought Richmond was one of the toughest places to work. "I guess it was because it was my home town, and Virginians tend to be slow to start on new things."

North Carolina physicians were friendly and seemed more willing to listen to his sales talks. "I soon found out that the people of North Carolina are different from the people in Virginia. Everybody was so friendly and just took you right in. Virginians are just as hospitable as North Carolinians, but they have to get to know you first.

"I remember the first night I was in a boarding house in North Carolina somebody wanted me to go to a party with them. I went because I was invited. That's so typical of North Carolina. You can get twice as much business out of North Carolina than you can in Virginia.

"It only took me two days to learn this about detailing in North Carolina. When you walked into a doctor's office one of the first things he would say to you was 'Are you going to the game this weekend?' and what he meant was the University of North Carolina game."

Claiborne replied, of course he was going, and he did. He knew that he would not be welcome in some of those doctors' offices if he couldn't talk Tar Heel football or basketball. "One of the things that impressed me down there was how sports-minded North Carolinians are," he said.

Texas and North Carolina had a lot in common, Claiborne recalled. "They take you for what you are and don't want to know who your ancestors were. If they like you they'll take you in almost overnight. Texas was a good market. I just loved working Houston. I could get more business out of Houston than Dallas."

For those few years before he was married, Claiborne lived out of a suitcase and was only home at Christmas. It was hard work and Claiborne made the most of his time.

"I wouldn't get in 'til about 6:30," says Claiborne, "and I would make about eight or nine calls. I made more than the average. The average man made about six. You had to wait for doctors. Of course, the busiest doctors are the ones you want to see. What you do is stick your head in the door a number of times during the day if you are in a concentrated area and just kind of gauge how many people are sitting around. If there are not too many people sitting around, then you wait. But if there are 16 people sitting there, then there is no use in waiting.

"The only way I was able to see as many as I did is just gauge the time. Sometimes I would ask the secretary. I would say, 'I've got to see doctor so and so because he is one of the most important men in town. Could you give me an idea when you are not quite as busy?'"

"I found that there are little tricks that you'd learn. Sometimes you found that a doctor who's supposed to take Wednesday afternoon off to play golf sometimes doesn't play golf. And I sometimes would come in on a Wednesday afternoon. The busiest people are the easiest to see, and it's true in the case of doctors you may have to wait, but as far as their willingness to see you is concerned, the busiest doctors are the easiest to talk to and welcome your visit because they want to learn the latest and want to have all the information they can get.

"The toughest doctors often were the ones who didn't have

much practice. They pretended to have a practice, but they didn't. I soon learned you could tell from the waiting room whether they were really busy. In Charleston and Savannah, where the doctors had night hours from 8 'til 11 in the evening, I worked until they quit."

Claiborne gained confidence quickly as he traveled across the country. The young detailman faced every day with new enthusiasm and excitement, striving to introduce his company to potential new markets.

"We had a very small business and we had a company that most doctors had never heard of. Some of 'em had heard of Robins Cascara. The thing about the business is that it's cumulative. If you have a product indicated in the right fields where the market is large, the wonderful thing about it is not that they've written the first prescription, but the refills.

"Some people will refill a product for 20 years. You get enough refills piled on, refilling and refilling, and then new prescriptions, and it begins to mount. The cumulative total can be quite large. We tried to get products that were of the type that are useful, that the doctor could use almost every day, which could be refilled."

Claiborne's hard work was paying off and Martha was confident enough by 1936 to make her son president of the company. The 26-year-old executive showed a good grasp of the business and a vision that would take the company to undreamed of heights.

"It never dawned on me that we would ever be a big company, as big companies go. I thought that we might get it up to a million dollars in gross sales, and that would have been pretty big, going from nothing. That was my dream, to get it to a million or a little more, but when we got to a million, it was to get it to $10 million, and then to $100 million and so on," he said.

To do that, however, Claiborne still had to take to the road to convince doctors to use Robins products while Martha did the office work and supervised the packaging and shipping operations.

To meet a growing work load, the company expanded, adding

Anthony Rose to its sales force, but not without sacrifice. As president of Robins, Claiborne was making $10 a week in 1937, while the salary of employee Rose was $25.

Claiborne strongly believed that a major key to success was the sales force, and he and others in the Robins organization in later years gave much thought to recruiting effective salesmen.

"You don't have to be a great salesman if you come across as

Office	NAMES	S	M	T	W	T	F	S	Total Time	Rate	Wages or Salary	Other Earnings	Total Earnings	Deductions O.A.B.	U.C.	Amount Due
	Martha J. Robins								44		15 00		15 00	15		14 85
	Alma May Robertson								44		12 50 ✓		12 50	13		12 37
	Gertrude J. Brooks								44		8 00		8 00	08		7 92
Selling	Week Ending Nov. 10, 1937															
	Anthony F. Rose								wk		25 00		25 00			25 00
	E. C. Robins								wk		10 00		10 00			10 00
Office -	Week Ending Nov. 20, 1937															
	Martha J. Robins								44		15 00		15 00	15		14 85
	Alma May Robertson								44		12 50		12 50	12		12 38
	Gertrude J. Brooks										8 00		8 00	08		7 92
Selling	Week Ending Nov. 17, 1937															
	Anthony F. Rose								wk		25 00		25 00			25 00
	E. C. Robins								wk		10 00		10 00			10 00

The weekly ledger Martha kept for the A. H. Robins Company in 1937.

believing in your product," he said. "We tried to determine motivation. It's a very difficult thing to do, but now and then you get a clue. For example, if you can get a guy who held down two jobs while he was in college you usually got a man who was motivated.

"Detailing is the same today. It's a little harder to get in because there are so many more companies with more men now, but it's still the same. It's like any other sales. If the doctor likes you better than the competition, he's more likely to write your product, assuming it has equal merit. You never, never know when you are going to hit the jackpot from one call. You could make a hundred calls and get very little in return, or you can make one call and the doctor likes you or something, and he writes your product. One doctor can make a heck of a lot of difference."

For Claiborne and A. H. Robins that difference came in the summer of 1937 while Claiborne was working Kansas City, Kansas. When he got into town he had followed his usual routine and asked pharmacists for the names of doctors who wrote the most business. One name came up on every list, Dr. P. M. Krawl.

"The only reason I'm here tonight is due to the greatest sales call that I ever made," Claiborne said in a speech to businessmen years later, in reference to Dr. Krawl. "He had the world's biggest practice, and I do mean he had it. It wasn't unusual to go by his office and see 250 people sitting there waiting. I had been told by all the pharmacists in town that if you could ever get Dr. Krawl to prescribe something, you had it made. And so I decided I was gonna see Dr. Krawl if I didn't see anybody else in Kansas City."

Claiborne was warned that Dr. Krawl was very difficult to see because he had so many patients. "I went by his office so often that the receptionist must have gotten tired of seeing me, because it was practically impossible to see the doctor. I tried and tried and tried to see him, maybe 15 times or more."

Claiborne spent his dinner money one day and bought the receptionist a nice box of chocolates. "Finally, the receptionist said that she would see that I got in to see him if I would come back just before 6 p.m., when they locked the door."

"There were still just gads of people," Claiborne recalls. "I brought a book and I sat there, and I sat there, and I sat there, and about a quarter to twelve there was one patient left, and I knew the time was coming. As soon as she came out I got a chance to see Dr. Krawl. He had his feet up on the desk."

THE DETAILMAN

Dr. Krawl looked tired after having seen patients for 15 hours. He said to the young salesman, "Tell me what you've got on your mind."

Claiborne replied, "I've got very little on my mind because I know you've had a full day. I'll make it brief."

So Claiborne told him about Donnatal. "That's all I took time to tell him. I didn't stay but a few minutes. I thanked him for his courtesy and left. I didn't say anything brilliant, I don't think, but the next day there is only one expression: all hell broke loose. Dr. Krawl had hit Donnatal and everybody that came in the door got a hundred Donnatal tablets.

"Well, Donnatal is good for most everything because most things are based on nerves, and Donnatal is good for nerves and gastro-intestinal disorders and spastic disorders. Well, we kept shipping him by air and every time they'd order 12 dozen that wasn't enough, so we shipped 24 and that wasn't enough, so we shipped 36 gross and that wasn't enough. Finally we got up to 60 gross. He was prescribing 95 percent, and it shows you that you don't have to hit the jackpot but one time.

"Dr. Krawl lived for at least 15 years and I was told by our men that when he died he was still prescribing Donnatal heavily. And the reason that this is so important is because at that time we had capital of only about $2,000, and when that ran out there wasn't any more. That was borrowed.

"Dr. Krawl alone, I figure, wrote enough in the way of prescriptions for us to put on several detailmen and to start spreading around the country. If he had not hit that night at midnight, well, we might not have even had a Robins Company."

"The miracle of Kansas City," as Claiborne termed it, was the one-in-a-million, hit-the-jackpot sales call. "That resulted in the eventual employment of 60 more salesmen to our sales force," said Claiborne. "If I hadn't seen Dr. Krawl that particular night, we would have made it, but it would have been three or four years later. I had the product that he wanted and suited most of his patients."

Claiborne's call on Dr. Krawl was not the only success an A. H. Robins Company salesman had. Other detailmen had great successes too. "I'm sure every man has had one or two extraordinary calls, but you might have to go a long time before that happens."

With the stakes so high for potential sales, Claiborne was a strong promoter of personal responsibility for salesmen in the field. "We said this to every salesman that came to us," recalled Claiborne. "You are the key to the future success of this company. You alone are because you are the one out there in the field facing the doctor and the pharmacist. We may be the best company in the world, but if you don't present us as the best company and do the best job, then we are not the best company in the eyes of that doctor, and they are the ones who are going to determine our future.

"We said that to 'em every time they came in here, and they knew that. They knew how we felt about the sales force. Most companies are no better than the people that are out there selling for them."

There were other doctors who wrote Robins products with great loyalty. One was Dr. Hudnall Ware, Sr. of Richmond. He grew fond of Claiborne and would always welcome him to hear the latest sales information.

"Dr. Hudnall Ware became a close friend and I called on him when I was detailing," Claiborne said, "but he did not write many prescriptions. But he did write a few things. He wrote for nausea, he wrote an iron preparation, and he wrote for vitamin B complex. It so happened we had three products in all three of those categories.

"I think we must have been the despair of other detailmen. Dr. Ware wrote all three: Donnatal, Allbee with C, and an iron product called Bironex. I doubt over the years, and that was a long time before he died, if he wrote a hundred prescriptions a month for anything else, and he probably wrote on the average of at least a dozen a day — I think I'm being conservative — for our products.

"So a dozen a day times 30 days, that's 360 prescriptions a month for our products. His children — two of them are doctors —

are still good friends of the company. How we happened to get Dr. Ware, I asked several doctors in town 'Who is the best OB doctor in town?' and they said, almost without exception, 'If I had a child, I would go to Dr. Hudnall Ware,' who was head of Obstetrics at MCV. So, I said, my goodness, this is the man I want." Claiborne was so impressed with those testimonials that Dr. Ware delivered all of the Robins children and several of the grandchildren.

In the Richmond business community fortunes improved as the city and nation recovered from the financial plight of the Depression. The city's economic situation was not as bad as in some other places in the country, particularly the industrial north.

Richmond's industrial volume gained 59 percent from 1929 to 1939, while the nation's dropped more than 16 percent. The tobacco industry, long a financial pillar for Richmond and the state, kept the city's unemployment from dropping as far as many other cities.

Richmond's early recovery and healthy financial position attracted companies from many other parts of the country, and as a result the city began to prosper in the late 1930s. The future of Richmond and the A. H. Robins Company looked better in 1937, and prosperity seemed within reach.

Claiborne's midnight call on Dr. Krawl was one of two events in 1937 that had a tremendous impact on his life. While detailing in Waco, Texas, he had another. He was introduced to Lora, the young woman who was to become his life's partner and share in the building of the Robins family and the A. H. Robins Company.

V

A WACO WEDDING

The doors to the offices in the Liberty Building in Waco, Texas were open on a sweltering June day in 1937 to help encourage any cool breezes. E. Claiborne Robins waited in a doctor's office to tell the physician about his products. He glanced through the door across the hall, where a young woman was seated at a typewriter.

Tired of reading, Claiborne got up and walked into the hall. He spent a few moments talking to the young secretary, then returned to the doctor's office.

Lora McGlasson, the young woman behind the typewriter, was still fussing to herself because her boss, who also happened to be her father, had told her she was to mind the office in the afternoon while he and her mother were away on a short trip. Lora had also wanted to go. She had completed all the briefs her attorney father had left for her, and she saw no need to keep the office open that afternoon.

Betty, the doctor's receptionist across the hall, needed an escort to a party that night and had asked Claiborne if he would like to go with her. "Certainly," said Claiborne, "I have nothing to do tonight." He had just written to a friend commenting that Waco "is the dullest town, nothing to do, I've seen all the movies and there is nothing for young people to do."

Betty had introduced Claiborne to Lora as "a very dear friend" and asked if she could bring him to a surprise party the two were having for a mutual friend. Lora agreed, so Claiborne went as Betty's guest.

"As it turned out," recalled Claiborne, "I didn't like the girl I was with at all. She obviously did not care anything about me. She just wanted to have somebody to take her to the party. Anyway, it ended up by my taking Lora home and the other girl went with somebody else. I don't know what happened to her, but it didn't matter because neither one of us had any interest in the other, so I took Lora home and started dating her."

"He took Betty to the party, but he brought me home and he's been bringing me home ever since," Lora laughed.

Claiborne fell in love on the spot. "I proposed to Lora on the second date, and she was smart enough not to accept immediately and told me that I should think about it for a year."

"If you still feel the same way at the end of a year, then we'll be serious about it," she promised, "but I think you had better go back to Virginia and see if I would fit in." Claiborne grinned and replied, "I know you will."

Lora was so excited about the new love in her life that she couldn't help telling her younger

Lora and Claiborne soon after they met in 1937.

brother, Irvy. He was the only family member home that weekend and he had met the young Virginian and liked him immediately. "Marry him!" he told Lora, when she bubbled over with the news of the proposal.

Claiborne suddenly found that Texas needed more coverage. "I discovered that there were more small towns in Texas than you could believe that needed to be worked, so I was circling around Waco for 150 to 200 miles for quite awhile," he chuckled.

Claiborne made Waco his base, going off to work in Dallas, Fort Worth and other Lone Star cities. He spent his weekdays detailing the Texas cities and towns but managed to get back to Waco by Friday nights to see Lora.

He arrived in town by 10 p.m., picked Lora up, and they went out for Cokes and hamburgers, or just for a ride around town in Claiborne's Ford. All Saturday was devoted to learning more about each other, and then Claiborne would leave Sunday afternoon for another week of detailing.

Claiborne spent the month before they were married detailing his products to doctors in Houston. He liked the city because, although the weather was hot and humid, doctors were receptive to him. Hotels were a bit expensive, so to save money he found a boarding house he liked.

"I had an attic room and two meals a day — breakfast and dinner — for $30. They were really good meals, too. The lady who owned the place just loved young people and she had a house full of them. She was a great cook and she wanted to see young people eat. Boy, did they eat! I don't see how she could possibly have made any money. I think she just did it because she loved young people. She had a big house and she must have had a dozen or more boarders in that house. I saved money for my honeymoon because the medical buildings were just a few blocks away, so I didn't even have to use my car. I bet I didn't spend two dollars on gasoline that month."

Lora's parents liked Claiborne. "He was such a Virginia gentleman," said Lora. She was concerned, however, about what Claiborne's mother would think about his involvement with a western woman. "Our lifestyle was a bit different in Texas, but we did have much in common." She worried that Martha would think that her only son would marry someone who would not appreciate him and his genteel ways.

The couple had similar backgrounds, however, and a similar cultural heritage. Lora had a college degree, had taught school for a year and was interested in music. She was a Baptist. Moreover, she shared Claiborne's dedication for work, earning money typing term papers and theses as a student at Baylor University. She thought the marriage would work, but she was uneasy about how she would be received back east.

A WACO WEDDING

Claiborne returned to Richmond with his heart and mind full of visions of life with Lora. He rarely called her, but during one call, at Christmas of that year, Martha picked up an extension by mistake. When she realized that her prospective daughter-in-law was on the line, she said in her soft Virginia drawl, "Lora, I'm so looking forward to meeting you."

Claiborne had told Lora that he had done a good selling job. "Mother will love you," he reassured her.

The first time Martha saw Lora was when Martha came to Waco for the wedding. "She couldn't have loved me or appreciated me more," said Lora. "We just hit it off."

Claiborne went to one of his largest prescribers in Waco, Dr. Bidelspach, to get a health certificate required for the marriage license. The physician looked at Claiborne and asked him if he was healthy.

"As far as I know, I am," said Claiborne. "You haven't been fooling around, have you?" was Dr. Bidelspach's next question.

"No sir," said Claiborne, "I'm not the fooling around type."

Dr. Bidelspach smiled and handed him the signed certificate without further comment. "Now that was trust," said Claiborne.

Claiborne and Lora had met on June 10, 1937 and were married by Dr. H. H. Hargrove on June 24, 1938 at Columbus Avenue Baptist Church in Waco. The church had recently installed a new organ, and the Robins-McGlasson wedding was the first at which it was to be played. Guests filled the church early and the ladies broke out demure fans as their men swabbed brows with handkerchiefs in the 97-degree Texas heat.

When the organist sat down

Lora on her wedding day and 26th birthday, June 24, 1938.

at the organ to start the service, however, he hit one note and the organ squeaked and wheezed to a stop. The wedding ceremony had to be accompanied with a piano, but the excited newlyweds regarded it as only a minor hitch in an otherwise magical day.

"The night we were married it was a very typical hot June day in Waco, and we were married at the Baptist church where she belonged," recalled Claiborne. "Somebody tipped us off that some of her brothers had decided that after the wedding they would plot to kidnap me for the night so they would interrupt our first night together.

"We decided we would foil that, so we went downtown and made a reservation at one of the local hotels, and immediately after the reception, which was held at the bride's home, we made a beeline for the hotel and we got there just before those that were pursuing us.

"There were only three major highways out of town, so they were stationed on all three highways to make certain we didn't get through. And, of course, we never came. So in that way our marriage got off to a success from the standpoint they didn't succeed in their kidnapping attempt."

The couple chose the Roosevelt Hotel as their refuge, but they were not to get off that easily. Irvy and some of the wedding party learned that Lora and Claiborne had a room on the top floor.

"They were not exactly sure where we were," said Claiborne, "but somehow they got an idea and somebody had gotten this powerful searchlight, and this powerful searchlight would go by the window every now and then."

The next day Claiborne and Lora headed northwest in Claiborne's new 1937 Ford on a grand tour of national parks. Travelers in those days had to rough it on occasion, and they spent their first night on the road in Pecos at a third-rate tourist court where there were no window shades and the shower was broken. Nothing, however, could spoil their happiness, and they faced whatever hardships may have occurred with a sense of adventure.

A Waco Wedding

Sometimes they went into a market to pick up something for lunch to eat at one of the many roadside tables built during the Depression by the Civilian Conservation Corps. Lora learned to take care of their household needs while traveling, sometimes doing the laundry in the bathtub of their efficiency apartment or motel, or sending Claiborne's shirts out to a laundry.

"I could have done them myself, though," she said. "My father and three brothers all wore white shirts. My mother taught me to iron them and not to have any 'cat's whiskers' in them, either."

Claiborne enjoyed a bit of detail work now and then as he and his bride learned to live together on the road. "Life is such fun with Claiborne," said Lora. She packed a "chuckbox" for snacks and they took rooms where they could find them. "We usually left in the mornings about 8:00 and traveled until we got tired or it was 5:00 or dark."

They dubbed their car "Josephine," and the Model A Ford chugged on through deserts and mountains as the newlyweds enjoyed their new life. They stopped at the Grand Canyon and arrived in Reno on July 4. With his characteristic good humor, Claiborne joked that he almost sent a telegram to friends saying, "Married two weeks and here we are already in Reno!"

They went on to Las Vegas and had dinner, noting how inexpensive it was. It was the first time Lora had seen "ladies of the evening" scantily dressed sitting in chairs on the side of the road. "I caught on pretty quickly. They were such painted dolls, all frizzed up. It was surprising in those days," she recalled.

They left Las Vegas about 8:00 that night and drove across the desert after sunset to avoid the heat and possible breakdowns. An hour after midnight they rolled into San Bernadino, tired and ready for bed. They took the first motel they saw and slept until 5:30 a.m. when the whole building began to shake.

The main line of the Southern Pacific Railroad ran right past the end of their room and one of the trains had come rumbling by.

"Every ten minutes, from 5:30 on, that place shook," recalled Claiborne. "All the trains came over the desert at night to avoid the heat. We finally gave up and went out and had an early breakfast."

They saw the Painted Desert and spent three days in Hollywood acting like two kids, taking the tour trips of the movie city. Claiborne managed to mix work with play, however, and picked up a detailman in Los Angeles who had contacted Claiborne by letter. He was hired on the spot to represent A. H. Robins on the West Coast.

When the honeymooners left the city they went through three national parks in California. As they neared San Francisco they noticed a steady stream of cars coming out of the city. When they got to their hotel they learned that San Franciscans left town every holiday and every weekend for the warmth of the desert.

"They have damp, chill air almost the year round," said Lora. "We went out sightseeing along the bay and were chilled to the bone. On the roof of the hotel it was so foggy we couldn't see anything."

The couple went on to Yellowstone Park, stopping one night and renting a cabin. "It was about 38 or 40 degrees that night," said Claiborne, "but there were logs in the fireplace and Lora soon had a fire blazing. Lora always did have a knack for doing those things better than I did."

They left Yellowstone and drove through Cody and Cheyenne, Wyoming. Claiborne needed to resume work, so they moved on to Denver. They set out to picnic one Sunday in Rocky Mountain National Park, looking forward to temperatures cooler than Denver's 90 degrees. At the top of the mountain it was 38. They settled for a grassy slope halfway down the mountain. Lora had managed to keep the food wrapped up and hot, and it was a tasty and scenic memory.

Denver doctors were friendly and open, so the couple decided to spend a month there. They found an efficiency apartment and paid $30 a month for rent and utilities. It was hot in the small apartment, but about 9:30 at night a breeze would come down from the mountains to cool things off.

One of Lora's goals during the honeymoon was to help her husband gain weight. The determined young Texan had wanted to be a dietitian and home economist in her teens, so the job was a joy.

"I only weighed 152 when we were married," remembered Claiborne, a lanky 6-foot, 2-inches. "I was skin and bones. My wife said, 'I can put weight on you.' And I said, 'It can't be done, I've been trying to put weight on for years.' She succeeded, and in three months I put on 20 pounds, and she did it by giving me pie a la mode of some kind every night.

"I had apple pie one night and I had strawberry pie one night. Fortunately in Denver, due to the coolness of the surrounding mountains, they have a proliferation of berries. You can get all kinds of berries all summer long in great quantities."

They moved on to Colorado Springs without mishap, except that a stalled car blocked the mountain road to Pikes Peak. This angered Claiborne, and according to Lora, it was the only time she ever heard Claiborne cuss. They spent the month of August in Kansas City, Kansas, where Claiborne had made his "jackpot" call on Dr. Krawl several years before.

"It was hot as blazes," they remembered, but, Claiborne said, "we were in love and just married so the heat didn't bother us that much." They found tennis courts close to their apartment on Troost Avenue and played often, in spite of the heat.

A famous swing band came through Kansas City in August and its performances became one of Claiborne's treasured memories. The band was led by Benny Goodman, who had put together some of the country's top swing musicians in a big band that had played Carnegie Hall in New York. It was an artistic triumph for the popular clarinetist and band leader, and he took the band on a tour that included Kansas City.

"Goodman had the most fantastic band at that time that's

ever existed, before or since," Claiborne said. He and Lora saw several performances, which featured Tommy Dorsey on trombone, Jimmy Dorsey on saxophone, Gene Krupa on drums, Teddy Powell on piano, and other popular jazz greats who went on to form their own bands.

"It was the most memorable occasion of jazz I have ever heard," exclaimed Claiborne. "People in the audience couldn't help getting up and dancing in the aisles."

In September, Claiborne and Lora returned to Richmond, where Lora was introduced to Claiborne's part of the world. Lora was a bit hesitant about coming to live in Richmond, knowing that societal customs could make it a bit cool toward outsiders. "But I was accepted with open arms because Claiborne was such a love," she said.

The Richmond custom of asking about one's father and mother and their occupations was a bit of an irritant to Lora because "Texans usually accept people for what they are now and not what their great, great grandpappy might have been." Claiborne was so well liked, however, that Lora was always treated respectfully. Genealogy was never an issue.

Martha Robins welcomed her new daughter-in-law with a warm heart and gracious manner, and Lora returned those feelings in full measure. "No one could have been more loving and helpful to a new bride in a strange city, and that wonderful relationship continued throughout her life," Lora said. "She made it so easy for me to become a part of her life and Claiborne's life."

"When we got back to Richmond," explained Claiborne, "we spent the first couple of months at my mother's home over on Rosewood Avenue near Byrd Park. Then we got a little apartment on Sheppard Street called Abbey View. It was right back of the Battle Abbey. The Catholic church was on the corner and the apartment is still there. We spent about two years at Abbey View. It was adequate until our first child, Betty, was born.

"I remember one thing about Abbey View: Of course nothing

was air conditioned in those days, and anybody that says it doesn't get hot in September ... well, I remember the hottest spell that I think I ever felt in Richmond. It went over a hundred every day for three days. It was September 27th, 28th and 29th in 1940. It was sweltering, Lora was pregnant with Betty, and the temperature went over 100 those three days."

Company business took most of Claiborne's attention, and Lora's enthusiasm for building the company matched her husband's. On the road during detail trips she traveled with Claiborne, kept them fed and handled the chores of traveling. As on their honeymoon, they got a small efficiency apartment if they were going to be in a location for three weeks or a month. At home she joined Martha and the other employees at the company counting tablets and putting them into bottles. Whatever was asked of her was accomplished with her usual efficiency and care.

Claiborne and Lora drove themselves hard to build A. H. Robins. Claiborne continued in sales and gradually built a competent sales team. Lora was in the plant working, talking to employees, and performing her duties as corporate secretary, even while she was pregnant.

On October 6, 1940, their first child was born, and they named her Lora Elizabeth. After Betty was born, Claiborne cut back on his detailing trips, leaving them to his expanding sales team. From then on he conducted the business from Richmond.

Soon the apartment was not large enough to handle their growing needs, so Lora and Claiborne spent weekends and evenings searching for a house. They found one at 5403 Bewdley Road in a pretty west end section called Glen Burnie. They bought the house in 1942 and lived there until 1948.

By 1942, increasing prosperity and the needs of World War II brought a new demand for drugs. That year, sales topped $100,000 for the first time. Prosperity returned to the country as the Depression years came to a close and war contracts put more money in the pockets of the populace.

Claiborne kept long hours at the company and spent more and more time in meetings for many civic and charitable affairs. He had joined the Rotary Club and was active in his church as he attempted to give back to his community some of his increasing good fortune.

When a son, E. Claiborne Jr., was born on August 9, 1943, and another girl, Ann Carol, came on October 1, 1945, the house on Bewdley Road became too small for three growing children, and another house was sought. Living in Richmond's west end, Claiborne had often passed a house situated on a wooded lot across River Road from the Country Club of Virginia. "No way I could ever afford that," he thought, but he had his eye on it when Lora began to discuss moving.

Left to right: Betty, Lora, Ann Carol and Claiborne Jr. in the late 1940s.

"A Mrs. Kirsten, one of the Mercurochrome heirs, owned it and was living there," recalled Claiborne, "but she had lived in Florida and she never quite got used to Richmond. I don't think she thought she was accepted enough for a person of her standing, and she had put the home up for sale. It was built by the Moseleys, I guess, at least ten years prior to the time that we bought it, which was in '48. We moved in, I remember, in January of '48.

"One thing I remember about it: We had just barely gotten

the last piece of furniture in the house and the moving van rolled out the gate and it started snowing. It was a beautiful sight to be in this new home with the fresh snow all over the place. We've been there ever since. We've always loved being there for the reason that it's ideal. When we sit out in our back sun room it's just like we are out in the country. We can't hear a sound."

His business a growing success, his home idyllic, and with three healthy children, Claiborne felt fortunate. "I was lucky in that," he said of his marriage. "I proposed to my wife on the second date. It shows you that impulsive decisions sometimes are pretty good," he laughed. "Maybe if you think about it too long you will change your mind. Since marriage is a pretty big gamble for everybody, it's always problematical as to whether it will last."

Lora embraced her married life fully and became increasingly involved in the social aspects of the company. "My wife has entertained in our home practically everyone in the organization, including a 500-man sales force, which is rather unusual," said Claiborne.

With help from the family maid, Martha Scott, Lora prepared shrimp Creole, usually by request. She also fixed ham biscuits and batter bread. A cherry-covered cheese cake was prepared by Dot of the original Dot's pastry. Claiborne and Lora received many fine letters of thanks from salesmen impressed with visiting the company president's home.

"I doubt whether there is any CEO in the pharmaceutical industry that's entertained everybody in the sales force over a period of years, and she did this herself," remarked Claiborne. "She wasn't asked to do it, she did it because she wanted to and she felt that it was important to maintain that close relationship between the sales force and the company. I think it was most effective, because everyone that was out there realized that this was very unusual. Many of the men that we entertained said they'd never even seen the chief executive much less been entertained by him."

Lora was also heavily involved in community affairs, as much as her duties as a mother would permit. "I think it is the mother's responsibility to take the children to the dentist or to the ballet or whatever they are doing," she said.

In addition to raising the children, Lora was a member of the boards of seven civic and service organizations, was committee chairwoman of another, and had memberships in four other civic and two social clubs. She was building committee chairman for the YWCA and chairman of the Y's building project steering committee.

Lora said she did not want to be a club president but preferred the role of "work horse," as she called herself. "Claiborne and I have been lucky to have the time and facilities to share," said Lora. "We're not put here on earth just to sit."

Her primary interest, however, was her family. "I enjoyed serving on those boards, but I tried to be home whenever Claiborne was home. He attended Rotary on Tuesdays, so I tried to schedule my activities around that."

When Martha Taylor Robins retired from the company in 1946, ending a 44-year career because of failing health, Lora began to take on more duties. She became secretary of the A. H. Robins Company and its subsidiaries and sometimes traveled with her husband.

Lora relieved her husband of the duties with the children as much as possible to free him up for business and social obligations. "My main desire was to keep him healthy and happy," said Lora. "We've never had a serious argument. We have disagreed a couple of times on the children's activities, but he made the decision, and it was all right. He has been a devoted husband and companion. I relish all the wonderful times we've had together."

"My wife has always been an important part of my business success," acknowledged Claiborne. "In the first place, she was very understanding at the amount of time that I spent, not only away from home, but in various functions that were connected either with the business arena or the civic arena. I did devote a lot of time to civic affairs, as most CEOs are more or less expected to be involved in the community and be active in everything that is worthwhile."

Through a solid marriage, Claiborne and Lora built a firm foundation. Claiborne could pursue his business with all the effort he desired, while Lora covered family needs. The results of this prized partnership began to show in a healthy profit curve that predicted the ultimate success of the A. H. Robins Company.

VI

A BILLION DOLLAR COMPANY

It would be very difficult, if not impossible, to build a pharmaceutical company from startup to a billion dollars in sales today, according to Claiborne.

"To get started today you would have to have an enormous amount of capital because you would have to have FDA approval, and if you were marketing a new chemical, a brand new chemical that was not established, you could easily spend $200 to $300 million to get it approved.

"In 1933 it was simpler. There was not so much supervision from the Food and Drug Administration, and you didn't have to have new drug applications if you used drugs that were known to be safe and effective, so there was not much expense in putting a new product on the market," Claiborne said. "We put several products on the market with virtually no cost.

"In those days we had our products manufactured for us by some of the better firms like Merck, Sharpe and Dohme, and Smith, Kline and French. We bought in bulk quantities of a million tablets at a minimum, so we did not have to have much capital. The method of selling is pretty much the same, with detailmen calling on physicians, medical advertising and direct mail."

Claiborne was selling hard in his first decade with the A. H. Robins Company, watching his budget and putting every penny back into the business. The falling fortunes of the A. H. Robins Company as he finished college had convinced Claiborne to keep a sharp eye on the balance sheet. He also never forgot the financial lessons learned in his early years as his mother, Martha, struggled with the family budget.

While he was denied nothing he needed, many frills and luxuries of life were often out of her financial range. As a result,

Claiborne was very conservative with the firm's money. If the funds were not in the company coffers, nothing was spent and nothing was built.

Frugality and hard work paid off. Gross sales in 1942 were far from the $1 billion the company would one day earn, but the $100,000-plus year was a significant achievement in the firm's history. The growing number of dollars in the company treasury gave Claiborne the courage to make the moves necessary for growth.

That year, for the first time, he

Claiborne in the 1940s.

felt comfortable enough with company income to begin building a sales staff. A friend called one afternoon to ask if Claiborne knew that the Richmond office of Charles Frost, a Canadian drug company, was closing. Claiborne realized that some good, professional salesmen would be looking for jobs, and he jumped at the chance.

Early the next morning, he knocked on the firm's door. "I'm Claiborne Robins of the A. H. Robins Company," he said to the secretary, "and I'd like to see the sales manager."

Ted Heffner already knew Claiborne and welcomed him. "Do you have any good salesmen?" Claiborne inquired.

"I have five, and three of them are pretty good," replied Heffner.

After the two men discussed the drug business for a while, Claiborne made his decision. He asked Heffner to come to work for him and to bring the three good men with him. The addition of the four new men doubled his sales staff, and Claiborne's judgment was correct. They more than doubled the company's sales in their first year on the job.

Claiborne's last year as a detailman on the road was 1940, when his first child was born. From then on he would run the

Claiborne and Ted Heffner stand in front of the company sign at 12 South 12th Street.

company from Richmond. His success in hiring good detailmen and seeing doctors as a detailman had proved fruitful, and orders poured back into the office.

By the mid-1940s, the growing company had too little space to package and ship its products. Claiborne rented new quarters at 12 South Twelfth Street, a two-story building with a basement that could accommodate his 20 employees.

"The company's meager beginnings were on 12th Street," remembered Vangie Windsor, a Robins employee hired in 1944, and who worked for the company 41 years. "There were just six of us on the first floor: Mr. Robins, his mother, Martha Taylor Robins, who came in every afternoon to work on the books, Mr. Heffner, my cousin, Iris Moore, Al Kenney, who joined the company a month after I did, and me.

"In the early days I would do my secretarial work sitting at a desk behind me in an open room separated from the shipping department by a filing cabinet backed up to shelves holding some A. H. Robins products. When the mail came, I would move to the other side of the office to do the billing on an old typewriter which belonged to Martha Taylor Robins. My cousin and Mrs. Robins occupied the only private office, the bookkeeping office."

By 1945 the post-war boom was just beginning, and the pent-up demand for products and services was pushing the national economy upward. Every day new opportunities seemed to open up. Claiborne began to think seriously about research, and a tip from one of his friends led him to hire A. H. Robins' first Medical Director.

A Billion Dollar Company

Dr. Eugene Jackson, an outstanding scientist, was teaching at Emory University in Atlanta and wanted to work in the private sector. He was hired in 1946 and served as the company's medical director. He soon played a significant role with A. H. Robins because he helped develop Robitussin, a cough medicine that would later become one of the company's most successful products.

"Dr. Jackson," said Claiborne, "wasn't actually an M.D., but he had a Ph.D. in pharmacology. He had taught at Emory University, so he knew a lot about pharmacy and pharmacological products."

Claiborne began thinking of overseas expansion in 1946, when he established his first foreign office in Puerto Rico. He hired Dr. Martin Reyes to begin building an overseas detail staff in Latin America, where A. H. Robins could be in on the ground floor of pharmaceuticals.

His administrative duties mounting, Claiborne needed someone who could handle some of the load. His old friend Mallory Freeman had returned from New York and was working in advertising at WRNL Radio in Richmond. They saw each other often, and Lora had become friends with Mallory's wife, Mary.

When Claiborne asked Mallory to come to work for A. H. Robins, Mallory was ready. He proved to be a great asset to the firm and handled advertising with expertise. Freeman also took an active role in Richmond's cultural life and was a performer in many of the area's theatrical productions.

"We have always been close friends," said Claiborne of Mallory. "Mary Freeman, Mal's wife, was a delightful person and a lot of fun to be with. She had a great sense of humor and could really see the good side of everything."

By 1948 Claiborne began to think seriously about building his own research department, convinced that Robins could never be a major pharmaceutical company without one. As usual, he would not commit money the company did not have, but healthy company earnings allowed him to hire a researcher, Dr. Robert Murphey, and put him to work in rented quarters at the University of Richmond.

Dr. Eugene L. Jackson, A. H.
Robins, Vice President and Medical
Director, 1953.

G. Mallory Freeman, A. H. Robins
Advertising Director, 1953.

Dr. Robert S. Murphey, A. H. Robins Chief
Research Chemist, 1953.

A Billion Dollar Company

"Dr. Robert Murphey, who was with us for many, many years, had a hand in developing Robaxin for us, and he started our first lab," said Claiborne. "We didn't have the money for a real lab. We rented space out at the University of Richmond and Dr. Murphey was in charge out there. I think we only had two employees, Dr. Murphey and one other. Dr. Murphey was excellent at contracting foreign firms and persuading them to perhaps let us have one of their drugs that they didn't have in the U.S. for us to market, and he was able to get several products from abroad.

"Bob Murphey's title was Scientific Development, but one of his main strengths was his unlimited energy and his ability to enjoy traveling. Everybody who went to Europe with Bob Murphey had their tongues hanging out because he knew the territory so well and he had all these people lined up before he left. He had met the top people in each company and they knew when he was coming, and he would sometimes make three countries in two days. He went over at least two to three times a year.

"One thing he did which was very smart, he made himself available and made them aware of the firm of Robins and the kind of excellent sales force it had and what we could do for a firm that would market a product here, and how we could concentrate on products when some of the big firms had so many products that they couldn't concentrate on any one.

"He kept up with the top scientific person in each company and kept up with all the literature that was published, and every time he would get something that he thought would be of interest to this particular company, he would send them a copy of the article. He was constantly feeding them material that was beneficial to them and they appreciated it. He had a wonderful relationship and therefore was very successful. I've never seen anybody who could seemingly travel with such relish and accomplish as much in such a short period of time as he did."

In 1948, cramped again by too-small facilities, Claiborne found another building at 1322 West Broad St. Again, more employees

The A. H. Robins Company located at 1322 West Broad Street in 1949.

were needed to handle the burgeoning orders. When the gross sales were totaled at the end of the year, the figure was over $1 million. Claiborne and Lora entertained a few friends at their new home to celebrate.

Sales in 1949 exploded with the introduction of Robitussin cough medicine, Pabalate for rheumatic affections, and Entozyme for digestive disturbances. They helped double the gross sales from the year before. Claiborne enabled the company to keep up with the demand. He streamlined procedures in the plant and hired more employees to keep the products moving. Sales soon topped $2 million.

"In 1949 was when we really took off," explained Claiborne. "We added Robitussin, that came through Dr. Jackson, who had read about the formula in a Canadian medical journal. We added another product called Pabalate for arthritis which no longer is in existence, but which, at that time, was current and considered good therapy. We added about three products in 1949 and 1950. That gave something besides Donnatal. Donnatal had been our primary product up until that time. By that time the volume was increasing so fast we were adding salesmen much, much faster. We were adding a dozen or more a year."

Claiborne knew why sales were growing. "We had products that a doctor could use daily. If a doctor had a fairly good practice, he could use one or more of our products a day. Another secret was that we had so few products that we could pound away at them, and that gave us an advantage."

Donnatal was key to Robins' early sales success because it was popular among doctors who valued its effect on nerves. Many health problems are based on nerves, and Donnatal is good for nerves, gastro-intestinal disorders and spastic disorders. In the early years the Robins sales team sold Donnatal almost exclusively.

"Donnatal, after we had it on the market for 15 or 16, maybe 20 years, was selling more than all the rest of the 500 competitors, or whatever we had out there, combined," said Claiborne. "It wasn't a thing in the world except maybe we were better salesmen, plus the fact that we were concentrating on it and the others couldn't afford to concentrate on it because they had other things they had bigger sales in that they couldn't afford to neglect in order to work the Donnatal formula.

"Small companies have that advantage. It's got to be a good product and it's got to get results, but any company that can afford to concentrate can make a product a big seller.

"I think it was the fact that we had products that doctors wanted and could use daily," said Claiborne of the company's early growth. "There are many products that are on the market that doctors have no opportunity to use more than once a month. Obviously, the sales potential is limited, but the kind of products we had — if the doctor had a fairly good practice — he could use two or three every day, several times.

"Not that we didn't have competition. The secret was we were able to just pound them. We didn't have that much. We didn't have 500 products to work, and we could just really concentrate on them. The old repetition, just bang, bang, bang. I think that was one of the secrets."

As the company grew, so did demands for more office, plant

The A. H. Robins Company offices and shipping facility at 1711 Ellen Road in 1950.

and shipping space. This was the continuing story as Claiborne met with his department chiefs, who pleaded for expansion. In 1950 Claiborne moved the company offices and shipping to 1711 Ellen Road, leaving the packaging operations at the West Broad Street facility. That move was remembered by one of Robins' early employees, Johnny Gordon, who was first hired in 1949.

"On Broad Street the room was already crowded. It had a low partition to define an aisle way from the front door back to the offices, and I got a desk and chair right in front of a plate glass window on Broad Street. It was either unbearably hot or very cold.

"After about a year there, Mr. Robins came in and announced that he had found us some space and that he was going to take the office staff up to Ellen Road. We were only there for a short period, but when we left we were so crowded that my desk was my card table from home. We did not have enough office space for any more desks, so I brought my own card table."

In 1951, knowing he needed more space for all of the firm's departments, Claiborne put up $150,000 to buy ten acres on Cummings Drive. "It seemed expensive at the time, but turned out to be a good buy," he said.

In 1952 Claiborne and his children break ground for the new company plant. Pictured from left to right: Dr. E. L. Jackson, J. E. Norton, Dr. W. R. Bond, Mrs. Norton, T. B. Robinson, Claiborne Robins Jr., Betty Robins, E. W. Zeller, D. H. Eason, E. Claiborne Robins, G. M. Kirkland, Ann Carol Robins, and J. E. Slater.

He hired The Austin Company, a firm that specialized in designing and building pharmaceutical facilities, to build the first A. H. Robins plant. The new building brought under one roof all operations, including laboratory, manufacturing, packaging, shipping and executive offices. Construction began in March 1952, and the Robins children helped Claiborne break ground with the first shovel of dirt at the ceremony.

The dedication of the new building was scheduled for April 1953, a year in which the firm marked the 75th anniversary of its founding. Although it was later found that the company was older than that, and had actually been founded in 1866, the gala dedication celebration eclipsed the error.

The idea for a grand anniversary celebration came to Claiborne during a trip to West Point with a small gathering of physicians from

Western Hemisphere nations who had been meeting in New York. During the trip, Claiborne visited with Dr. Louis H. Bauer, then president of the American Medical Association, who told Claiborne that he wanted to hold a Western Hemisphere conference of medical men, but had dismissed the idea because of the expense.

Claiborne's New York public relations agency got wind of the idea and came up with a plan to celebrate the 75th year and dedication of the new Robins building while simultaneously holding the medical meeting in Richmond.

It was a daring idea, especially since A. H. Robins would pick up all the expenses. Claiborne knew it would cost hundreds of thousands of dollars, almost all of the profits of 1952, but the more he thought about it, the more he liked the gamble. Company sales were surging forward and Claiborne speculated that the publicity resulting from the conference would create goodwill with the doctors that could be worth millions in sales of Robins' products. Several weeks after their meeting, Claiborne called an astonished Dr. Bauer to announce his plans and to begin organizing the medical conference.

Claiborne in 1953

The new $1.5 million building was completed in December and the company moved into the building on New Year's Day 1953. The dedication of the building and the first Western Hemisphere Conference of the World Medical Association were scheduled for April.

The dual events proved an astounding success, far better than Claiborne had expected. Physicians from every state in the nation, and 600 from 20 South American countries, came for the conference. Newspapermen from across the country spent the week in Richmond, and millions of readers learned through their publications that the conference was sponsored by the A. H. Robins Company. Virginia Governor John Battle welcomed the guests, and they toured Richmond and Williamsburg.

"Mr. Robins had thought it would be great publicity for the company to host the conference," recalled Johnny Gordon. "So he extended the invitations and so forth and here we had all of these people from North and South America arriving in Richmond and he had booked the Jefferson Hotel and our office staff had been forewarned.

"He had asked us to be sure to try to do whatever we could to make the thing go real well. We had an office staff that was very small, and in order to man the conference and keep the office going, we had a Jefferson schedule and an office schedule. So we worked one place for about five hours, then we'd rush to the office, so we really had long days.

"And he had gotten a couple of public relations people from New York who happened to be a husband and wife team, Harold and Billy Coy, and what Harold couldn't think of, Billy could, to really challenge the local yokels. They really had us strung out the whole time, but we managed to do what I think was a really good job. We really got a lot of mileage out of that."

To give the conference added flair, the A. H. Robins Company invited some special guests. The governor of each state was asked to nominate a distinguished doctor in his state to attend the meeting. The only requirement was that the doctor be 75 years of age in keeping with the 75th anniversary celebration.

Astonishingly, 47 physicians came and they added much flavor to the meetings. In spite of some concern that there might be medical problems among the older guests, there were none, and all the guests expressed their appreciation for the hospitality shown by Claiborne, Lora and their staff.

"It's hard to put an exact figure on it, but we received millions of dollars of publicity from that meeting," Claiborne said. "Those 47 older doctors went home and told all their colleagues and friends about it. A. H. Robins certainly benefited tremendously from that meeting in 1953."

Another more subtle, but effective advertising program began in 1954, when a friend in the printing business brought Claiborne a little publication tailor-made for A. H. Robins. The "Robins Reader" featured inspirational messages and articles on such diverse subjects as youth and marriage, and technical information on the medical and pharmaceutical professions.

Written by Gerald H. Bath, the little quarterly was sent to thousands of doctors, dentists and veterinarians across the country. The covers, which were usually scenes of countryside, soft and gentle, and which fit smoothly into the magazine's inspirational theme, displayed original art by Frank Mann, the company's talented assistant advertising director.

Claiborne liked the publication because he felt it conveyed the spirit of the employees and the company. Over the years, many doctors praised the value of the publication and indicated that they sometimes used it as a teaching aid in Sunday School. Thousands of letters were received each year complimenting the "Robins Reader." Claiborne was sure that it played a significant part in creating the image of A. H. Robins as a company that cared about people.

Richard Velz, a public relations expert, came to work for Robins in 1958 and created some of the company's best ideas for promotion. He gained Claiborne's confidence and soon was handling much of his civic and business duties. "The boss works all the time," Dick Velz marveled in a March 1960 article about the company in *The Commonwealth* magazine. "I never had a boss like this before. No golf. No yacht. No Mediterranean cruises. Just a little bit of baseball, a lot of good deeds — and back to work again." Dick and his wife, Anya, became friends with Claiborne and Lora, and were often guests on vacation trips.

Claiborne was alert to any capable person or innovative plan to promote the A. H. Robins Company, but he always had his eye on the balance sheet. He scanned every financial document produced in the company and could spot the smallest error. His reputation for a keen eye led to one of the legendary stories told in the company about him.

One afternoon in 1959 he made his rounds of the company after 5 p.m. and came into the order department where the day's orders were being processed. Bob Watts, a new employee, was startled when he heard a voice. "Hello, Bob, I'm Claiborne Robins," and Watts was impressed that the company president knew his name.

Claiborne picked up a stack of orders that had come off the processing machine and spotted an error in the amount of discount to which the customer was entitled. He asked Watts to correct it the next day. The incident gave credibility to Claiborne's reputation for an almost uncanny ability to find errors. The story that swept through the company was that Claiborne had told Watts to "stop that computer, that number is wrong."

Watts laughed: "There's no question that Mr. Robins is a very good reader and observer. He can look at a piece of paper and go to the point right away. But at that time we didn't even have a computer." Still, the story persisted, and at the end of 1959 the most important number was not only correct, it was encouraging: $33,393,120 in sales; another company record.

Claiborne's instinct for marketing kept him constantly searching for more ways to keep A. H. Robins products before physicians and pharmacists. In the 1950s Claiborne's salesmen sponsored dinners for residents and interns. It was a time when those entering the medical profession were paid very little, and Claiborne felt they would appreciate a good meal more than a medical bag or a stethoscope.

There was no sales pitch from Robins, just a drink, dinner and conversation, but the doctors would remember Robins later when they got into medical practice. "We just wanted to say that we appreciated the hard work they were doing," said Claiborne.

When his advertising staff brought him a proposal in 1959, he quickly agreed to it. The idea was to run ads focusing on doctors, pointing out the years of sacrifice and study it takes to become a doctor. The ads would not push Robins products; rather, they were intended to draw attention to the important work doctors do and the effort it takes to become one.

The series was entitled "Doctor of Tomorrow" and would run in national magazines. Claiborne was enthusiastic about the ads, and the company took double-page spreads in the medical journals. The ads were popular with the doctors, and the company ran them for 11 years, with great success.

In March of 1960, Claiborne built a third addition to the Cummings Drive plant, adding 50,000 square feet of space for warehousing. A. H. Robins de Mexico and a new Canadian plant were added to the foreign division in that year. Dimetapp, a cough medication, was introduced in December, and company sales totaled more than $37 million at year's end.

The company needed more office space, and in April of 1961 a new six-story office tower was opened, just one month before

The Robins family breaks ground for the office tower addition in April 1960 while company employees look on. Left to right: Claiborne Jr., Betty, Claiborne, Lora and Ann Carol.

Claiborne's 25th anniversary as company president. In 1962 A. H. Robins continued the headquarters expansion by purchasing a 44,000-square-foot building across the street from the main plant. Also, ground was broken for a new research center.

Company sales topped $50 million in 1963, one of the most significant years in the firm's history. The $2.6 million research center opened in February of 1963,

Claiborne poses on a tractor during construction at Cummings Drive.

with Governor Albertis Harrison as the guest speaker. The research center was staffed by about 40 scientists and technicians. In later years, it was enlarged several times and employed more than 350.

Meanwhile, the sales staff was growing, as were sales. "Every year we kept adding men," said Claiborne. "We got up at one point to where we had 650 detailmen on the road. That's a very expensive thing, of course, to pay salaries and travel and all of that, but we supported that many. Of course, as we kept adding more we kept growing.

A. H. Robins corporate offices and manufacturing facility at 1407 Cummings Dr.

"I am sure that one of the reasons that we were so successful at getting employees, salesmen and scientists was the fact that we had a reputation all over the country of being a fine firm to work for," said Claiborne. "It was a marvelous thing because we were able to get the best. We could pick and choose. We always had a waiting list in practically every category. We could pick the best that was available. This came because of word of mouth from our own employees and salesmen."

Claiborne began to diversify the company in 1963, first buying Morton Manufacturing Corporation, the firm that produced Chap Stick lip balm. One of the more significant events of that year was the decision to make a public offering of company stock. It was a tough decision for the family, as it would no longer be the sole owner of the company, yet it made good business sense.

In March 1963, 350,000 shares were sold to the general public and 75,000 shares were sold to employees at a discount. A second offering of 400,000 shares was made available in March 1965. In those two years, sales jumped to $65 million.

"It was customary for the CEO of the company who was going public to be present," remembered Claiborne, "so I went up and I bought, officially, the first 100 shares of A. H. Robins that were traded. I think I paid $69 for it, and I still do have it somewhere, that 100 shares framed," he chuckled. "I met Keith Funsten, the head of the NYSE. They entertained me at a luncheon in their boardroom right after we had been on the trading floor. It was very interesting being on the trading floor — it's managed chaos."

From his vantage point among the traders, Claiborne recalled the day in 1933 when he and Martha had borrowed $2,000 from Central National Bank in Richmond to keep the family business alive. There had been some tight budget years through the 1930s, but the A. H. Robins Company had come a long way since those hard and uncertain times.

Claiborne wasn't about to rest on his laurels, however, and he

Claiborne (center) visits the New York Stock Exchange for the first public offering of A. H. Robins stock.

focused on foreign acquisitions. George Thomas joined the company in 1965 as Director of International Development. With his help Claiborne began to expand the company's international holdings at a much faster pace. Sales at the end of 1966 totaled more than $74 million.

"In France we bought two companies, and in Germany we bought two companies," said Claiborne. "We retained the management in most cases because they were the founders of the company and they had an interest. We gave them an incentive. By retaining the original owners, they had a pride in what they had accomplished up to the point that they sold it, and they had a certain amount of pride in continuing to make it a good investment for us.

"George Thomas, who was our Vice President of the international area, was responsible for most of these purchases. He was fluent in several languages and came across these companies. I don't know exactly how he came up with them, but they were mostly companies that he discovered and we took a look at it and decided to buy them, and most of them turned out pretty well. We didn't make any tremendous sums because they were not large companies, but we made profits in all of them for awhile.

"Bob Murphey was our rolling ambassador abroad. He was a scientific man himself and made some wonderful contacts with Europe, and we got several products, particularly Reglan, from Europe, and that turned out to be a major product for us. We kept adding products like Dimetapp, which turned out to be very successful, and we added several new forms of Donnatal and several new forms of Robitussin.

"We had one woman who was Iranian. We had built up quite a business there, and when our plant was shut down by the regime because it was an American plant, we wondered if we were going to get any further business from Iran.

"We continued to get business for quite awhile because we had somebody who was Iranian and she would slip in and go to the customers who bought our products and they would give her orders and we'd ship them out of England. They didn't come from America, so they would accept them at the port of entry coming from England, so for years afterwards we shipped quite a bit of stuff into Iran, even after we had lost our plant. The doctors wanted the products.

"We bought a small company in Brazil. I went down there one time. It was a very nice little company, but the problem in Brazil, we never made any money. I'm so amused every now and then when I read that Brazil is the country of the future, and they have been saying that every 20 years for the last 60 years," chuckled Claiborne.

"The reason that you can never make any money in Brazil is that inflation is rampant. The medical board down there puts a ceiling on what you can charge, and then inflation just runs away with you like 200 percent in one year, and they'll give you a 10 percent increase or some such ridiculous thing. So there is no way you can ever make any money in Brazil, as we found, due to inflation.

"In Great Britain we started out from scratch, which is the hard way. We started out without a nickel. We established a branch office and we had the products manufactured for us, and we put on

Claiborne in the early 1960s.

a sales force and started out detailing. Obviously, that was much slower. Eventually it turned out to be profitable, but it took eight or ten years before we were able to turn out.

"Great Britain is not an easy market to break into because you've got two handicaps. We were completely unknown when we started. Plus, the fact that you have the health system there, doctors don't like to buy anything that isn't one cent a thousand. I mean, they want the cheapest possible thing. It doesn't matter whether it's the best; they want the cheapest.

"Many of the things were not on the prescribed list by the government. So the way we got some of our business was that most of the doctors over there practice privately at night. They do that because they don't make enough off of the health system to justify being in practice, and most people who had any money at all would go to the private doctors at night because they didn't have to have 200 people in line ahead of them."

Robins' acquisitions were so successful that by the time Claiborne was to step down as president in 1975, the company had established more than 15 subsidiaries worldwide and marketed its products in more than 100 countries.

Although A. H. Robins was very successful in the pharmaceutical world, Claiborne kept moving toward diversification. He wanted the company to be in a good position if the pharmaceutical industry became less profitable or if its ability to operate became hampered by pending government restrictions.

The Morton Manufacturing Corporation acquisition in 1963 had proved profitable, and in 1967 Claiborne bought two other companies to expand Robins' consumer operations: The Polk Miller Products Corporation which produced Sargeant's pet products, and Parfums Caron, a French perfume maker.

"Caron got to be kind of a drag; that never did pay in the U.S., even though it was highly respected," explained Claiborne. "Caron is considered probably one of the three top perfumeries in France. In the U.S. it never got a foothold because there are about 10,000 competitors. The U.S. market is no place to go into the perfume business, I can tell you."

Morton Manufacturing and Polk Miller were combined into a new subsidiary, Miller-Morton, in 1968 and became a significant profit maker for the company. The company's profits continued to soar, reaching $100 million in 1967.

As the company grew, so did the pressures on its CEO. Claiborne's pace in 1970 was horrendous. Betty Brown, who came to work for him that year, recalls: "I could not believe that schedule. It was nothing for him to have over 100 meetings a week. It was all we could do to get him where he had to be."

Claiborne agreed: "It was hectic and probably stupid, but I was involved in so many things. I was gone three and four nights a week, and tried to be home on weekends. I made that choice because, if you were a head of a company and a civic leader, that was expected of you.

"Maybe I neglected my family to some extent, and bless her heart, Lora raised the children. But they turned out all right and they seem to have a great deal of regard for me, so I guess they haven't held it against me too much," he mused.

Bowing to the pressures, Claiborne relinquished some of his responsibilities in June of 1970 and became Chairman of the Board. He turned over the duties of the president to the company's long time legal counsel, William L. Zimmer III. It was helpful, but his schedule as chairman was still very heavy.

Claiborne felt uneasy one May morning in 1972, and a pain in his left shoulder and arm became more persistent. Then the pain intensified and moved into his left jaw. Alarmed, he called Dr. Burke and told him of his problems. Dr. Burke examined him and immediately called the emergency medics. They rushed Claiborne to St. Mary's hospital where they confirmed his fears. He had suffered a heart attack. His incredible pace and the pressures of his work had caught up with him.

Claiborne's doctors told him that he had to cut down on his schedule or he wouldn't be around much longer. "I got the message," he said. Although he did not stop his company work, he did cut down on outside meetings and duties.

In May of 1973, almost a year to the day since his first heart attack, Claiborne was relaxing at his Virginia Beach house when he felt pain in his jaw again. Lora rushed him to the hospital, but they found no evidence of a problem. To be on the safe side, they kept him overnight for observation. The next day, after more tests, the diagnosis was clear: another heart attack, but milder than the first.

In his hospital bed, the reality of his own mortality made Claiborne consider more urgently the need for a plan for his family and the company for the time when they would be without his leadership. He was also forced to curtail his myriad activities.

"I cut back," he said. "I'm not exaggerating; that was 150 meetings. I was including things I enjoyed. I decided that I would just not go to Rotary 52 times a year. I still went a few times a year, but I cut that out considerably. I cut out executive committee meetings. There were a lot of civic meetings at night that I cut out, things that I used to go to, like chamber of commerce and many other civic endeavors.

"By eliminating all of these side meetings, I was able to reduce my schedule by at least 50 percent. I didn't stop doing things, but I just didn't push myself, and if I felt tired, I just didn't go. My heart attacks undoubtedly came from two things: I put on some weight, which certainly didn't do me any good, and I had just been going at an incredible pace, day and night."

For 40 years his unwavering energy had led the firm from a

tiny family company near the bottom to the very top of the business world. Claiborne knew he had exhausted much of his physical strength to maintain the demands of running the company, and he wanted the leadership to remain in the family.

His father's heart attacks had a sobering effect on young Claiborne Jr. His interest in sports waned and he stepped up his participation in the business. The young man had made good progress through the ranks, but at 29 he had not yet gained the experience needed to head a multi-national company, nor had he demonstrated the drive and dedication so clearly a part of his father's personality.

William Zimmer, a brilliant legal mind who had been named company president in 1970, was named CEO in 1975, when Claiborne turned 65. Zimmer, however, was nearing the end of his career, so he filled the top executive's job until Claiborne Jr. could gain the experience to take the post. Zimmer retired in 1978, and Claiborne Jr., at 33, was named President and Chief Executive Officer of the A. H. Robins Company. Claiborne, however, still remained chairman of the board.

There was speculation in the financial community about the management capability of A. H. Robins with Claiborne Jr. at the helm, but the young chief executive gradually put those

E. Claiborne and E. Claiborne Jr. in the early 1980s.

suspicions to rest as the company continued to expand its international operations and increase sales. When Claiborne Jr. became chief executive, Robins sales had reached $357 million. Eleven years later, at the time of the sale of the company in 1989, sales were almost a billion dollars.

Claiborne Jr. expressed his feeling about following his father as chief executive in an interview with *The Commonwealth* magazine in June of 1982: "I have tremendous respect for my father. Tremendous respect. When I took over as president, one of my goals was not only to take over what he put together, but to build on that and make it even better. And I do not take that as a challenge to be better than my father. But I have a tremendous respect for what he did, and my desire is to carry on that same drive, that same success."

Claiborne Jr., who once had dreamed of a professional sports career, had grown into a responsible business executive who led his company with good judgment and an appreciation for the work his father had done over the years. The work of three generations had successfully built the A. H. Robins Company into a billion dollar business.

VII

"WORLD'S BEST BOSS"

Building the A. H. Robins company into a billion dollar concern required capable vision and occasional risk taking, both of which Claiborne demonstrated. The ultimate success of the company, however, could not have been achieved without the unwavering commitment of its employees.

Claiborne's ability to enlist his workers' loyalty, trust and dedication to the company became the true mark of his leadership. With his friendly, outgoing personality and a rare generosity of spirit, Claiborne established a rapport with his employees based on mutual respect and a shared aspiration for success.

"I think it comes to me from making people feel their job is important," reflected Claiborne. "The problem is that most bosses are so busy they don't get around to telling individuals ... that they are doing a good job. As a result, they feel like they are left hanging and they wonder how they are doing.

"I've tried to let people know that they are appreciated and that they are important, ... that they exist," said Claiborne. "In a big company that is important. I feel that we got greater productivity, greater loyalty, and more demand for jobs at Robins. We never had problems getting good people; our own people spread the word."

Nita Winston, a 16-year veteran in the International Division, and a friend of the author, recalled how Claiborne would thank employees in the annual report with the following statement: The greatest asset a company can have on its books is the people. "That is your Granddaddy," she said. "I tell people that they don't know what it is like to work for a company and truly be appreciated as a person unless they have worked for E. Claiborne Robins."

Claiborne was steadfast in his dedication to the company, and he asked the same from each employee. They responded in kind, and it was that relationship that made A. H. Robins the success it became during Claiborne's 50 years of leadership. From the beginning, the self-reliant and ambitious Claiborne took naturally to the role of leader.

"To lead, you've got to inspire people to do a better job, and one way to inspire them is to let them know that you are aware when they do a good job. Of course, if they do a poor job you've got to let them know too, but you do it in a diplomatic way. Somebody told me one time that when I fired them that it was the nicest firing they ever had," he chuckled.

Claiborne sharpened his executive skills by facing new demands every day, and he thrived on the challenge. He hired the best people he could find and then stimulated them to achieve levels that may have been higher than even they had expected.

"I tried to run the company as I think a company should be run," explained Claiborne. "I tried to get good people who ran their own departments, and while they reported to me, as long as they ran them well, there wasn't anything much to do with them. I just kinda was there in case there were any problems.

"I concentrated more of my efforts in the sales area and in the personnel area. I found that while I was not Personnel Director, if any problems ever came up in personnel eventually they ended up in my lap. That maybe was my fault, but I tried to keep the morale of the employees high. I felt that was one of my duties, and I worked on that."

A. H. Robins Company employees felt like a family, with a leader who made it a point to be accessible, and who expressed his appreciation and concern for their problems.

"My door is open to anyone," Claiborne once explained to his secretary when she tried to protect her boss against the demands on his time.

"If they came without an appointment I might have had to schedule them later," he explained, "but I saw them no matter who they were. I don't think I turned anybody away over the years,

Claiborne in his office in the 1970s.

salesmen or otherwise, and I think it paid off. It was amazing what I could learn from someone."

A top-notch sales force was crucial to the success of the company, and Claiborne led one of the best in the pharmaceutical industry. "I am sure that one of the reasons that we were so successful at getting employees, salesmen, and scientists, was the fact that we had a reputation all over the country for being a fine firm to work for," said Claiborne. "It was a marvelous thing because we were able to get the best. We could pick and choose. We always had a waiting list in practically every category. We could pick the best that was available. This came because of word of mouth from our own employees and salesmen.

"I guess we violated all the so-called Harvard Business School rules," he laughed. "We never employed anybody from Harvard. They were really overtrained and sometimes trained so methodically that they missed the point of what they were doing."

Selecting good salesmen to represent A. H. Robins was critical to the company's success, and Claiborne used whatever resources were available.

"I enlisted the pharmacist sometimes and asked if there were some good men in the area. And if the answer was yes, we would approach the man and tell him about the company, that it was small and there was potential for opportunity and growth, and if their company wasn't recognizing them for their hard work they should work for Robins. They would be paid as well as any company in the industry would pay, and we frequently paid higher than they thought.

"It paid off because a man that is good can pay for himself in a short period of time. We paid salary and commission. We didn't do that for the lifetime of the company, but when we started we paid salary and commission. We did have incentive and, of course, we gave them mileage on their car. They did have to own their own car. We didn't give them a car at the time. We couldn't afford it. Later on, of course, we gave them all automobiles, but that was much later."

Though he had no formal sales training, Claiborne spurred his sales force with stories of the value of hard work.

"I told a story to our sales force many times that I think is very, very appropriate to life," said Claiborne. "It's a baseball story. In baseball there are only a very few hitters in the big leagues who average over .300 for the year, and they are the ones who make the big salaries that you read about in the headlines. There are hundreds of others who don't do so well, who average .250.

"Have you ever thought about how little difference there is between the stars and the guys who hit .250? There's only one extra hit out of every 20 times at bat. If you're at bat 20 times and get six hits every 20 times, you're a .300 batter. If you get five hits every 20 times, you are a .250 batter.

"There is such a tiny gap between those who are really the top winners and those who are just mediocre, and that is so true of life. The ones who just really put out a little, just a little bit extra, and the ones who just give it a little bit more enthusiasm and attention are the ones who get way ahead.

"I told our sales force that if you made one extra call a day, just one extra call more than your competition, then over a 20-year period you would gain two years on your competition. And I ask you, who in life wouldn't like to have a two-year head start in a race? If you couldn't win with a two-year head start, then you don't deserve to win.

"If more people realized what an extra hour a day means to the long-term success of a person, they would do it. They don't realize what that inch-by-inch progress amounts to over a period of years. If a person really works hard, his boss will notice, his supervisors will notice. He may not realize it at the time, but the extra effort now may affect his promotion ten years in the future. It's going to pay off."

Claiborne lived his philosophies as he built A. H. Robins, inch-by-inch. He also created goodwill, and that became an enduring aspect of the Robins story as many employees considered themselves part of an extended family.

No one understands that better than Vangie Windsor, who worked at Robins for 41 years. Over four decades she developed a close rapport with Claiborne and the family, beginning when the company was still in its infancy.

"I watched the family grow and the company grow into one of the most respected companies in the pharmaceutical industry, or any industry, for that matter. The company has come a long, long way, but Mr. Robins has remained the same to me, a man most appreciative of what he has and always willing to give to others part of the glory.

"I remember the first $1,000 order we received. I practically screamed, and Mr. Robins came running over wanting to know what was wrong, so we all rejoiced over that. I think that was 1948, after Pabalate was introduced.

"Mr. Robins always wanted everyone to be treated equally.

When we moved up onto Ellen Rd., the packaging department stayed at 1322 West Broad, so he said that he wanted us to mingle with those girls and make them feel like they were a part of the company, too.

Vangie, like many Robins employees, came to appreciate her boss, not only as the man who signed her paychecks, but as a person.

"He was so much fun to be with," she explained, "so down to earth. You never felt you couldn't say anything. I worked with Marshall, his secretary, right outside his office, and if we were laughing about something he would stick his head out and say, 'Did I miss something?' It was like we were working for our company — not for him, but with him.

"I remember one day — there were three of us in the office at that time, this was down on 12th Street — and Mr. Robins started telling us this joke, and Mr. Heffner came downstairs and Mr. Heffner did not like jokes in mixed company, and he let it be known. We left Mr. Robins standing in the floor and went back to our desks.

"We thought afterwards, well, you know, Mr. Robins owns this company and we left him standing. So he came back individually that day and told each one of us the end of the joke. I can't remember the joke, but I remember the punchline: 'Who put the Novocain in the Vaseline?'"

With an unrelenting drive to maximize the company's stature, Claiborne kept planning, always looking ahead, and his executives soon learned that the boss always had his eye on the future.

Having a good secretary, Claiborne was able to keep ahead of things, and no one was more appreciative of a good secretary than Claiborne. "An efficient secretary can really make a difference," he said, "and I was blessed with the best of them." They were Marshall Phillips, Betty Parker, and Betty Brown.

"The important things in any businessman's life or anybody's life, for that matter, is a good marriage and a good secretary or executive assistant," said Claiborne. "If you've got those two, you've got it made."

Claiborne's first secretary was Marshall Phillips, who came to work for Claiborne in the 1950s. She was an attractive, outgoing blonde with big eyes, and her sense of humor and cheerful demeanor helped project the company image of friendliness and efficiency. Claiborne's increasing workload required more help in his office, so Betty Parker came to work in the late 50s. Betty Parker was warm and dedicated.

Betty Brown was promoted to Claiborne's office in 1970 after working for ten years in other positions in the company. With a flair for handling people, Betty Brown quickly earned Claiborne's praise.

"Of course, Betty Brown has been with me 22 years and she is a jewel and I have been so fortunate because she has been able to handle everything and she knows exactly the routine.

"I don't have to tell her but once, and to have an assistant of that caliber means so much. I can't express adequately how important that has been, because it has enabled me to do not only the things in the civic area, but other things I couldn't have done if I didn't have someone that was capable. Betty can write a letter for me, and it is a rare situation when I have to make any changes," he said.

Betty Brown stayed with Claiborne throughout his years with Robins and beyond, transferring to his retirement office as his executive assistant. For over 20 years she has been invaluable to Claiborne, handling most of his personal affairs.

Even on his busiest days, Claiborne was always pleasant and cordial to his secretaries. Marshall Phillips liked to tell of the occasion when Claiborne called her into his office to dictate a quick letter before rushing off to a meeting and, in a hurry, she sat on Claiborne's hat.

"I was late that morning and he was waiting for me, so I grab up my book and I go in like I may be late but I'm efficient, and the next thing I know I'm pulling out this absolutely flat hat. He

Claiborne with his Cadillac.

never said a word. I'm all apology. Ordinarily, when he went to lunch he'd take his hat and put it on when he got out of the elevator and out the front door. Well, that day he walked out going to lunch with his hat perched on his head and it was all back like it should be. There are not too many secretaries that can come in and sit on their boss' hat and you would never have known I had done a thing.

"He used to tell me, 'Those who don't make mistakes never do anything.' Well, I did more things than anybody had ever heard of. Sometimes I can think back and wonder why in the world he put up with me. I was a good secretary, but I could do some real off-the-wall things, like pulling a whole file cabinet full of flowers down on the floor, and all he said when he came out was, 'What are you doing out here walking in all that dirt, Marshall?'

"Mr. Robins got a new Cadillac and we were so excited about the Cadillac that he took us — it took two trips — all the secretaries two or three blocks for a ride in the Cadillac, which we had never been in before. They were the kinds of things that bosses don't ordinarily do. You could play with Mr. Robins. He wasn't, 'I am the boss.'"

Claiborne's balanced disposition and good humor were legendary and a primary reason employees stayed with the company. "I've never seen him lose his temper," said Betty. "I've seen him a little annoyed, but I've never heard a word in anger. He just never got upset. And he has a wonderful sense of humor. I love to hear him laugh. He was such an inspiration to all of us."

Laughter was part and parcel of company Christmas celebrations, with Lora occasionally enjoying the festivities as well. As Marshall Phillips remembered, "Mr. Robins always popped the cork on the first bottle of champagne, and we had some great parties. He made it a point to dance with each of the girls — and we were girls then — and he gave our bonus checks out at the party. We all got a kiss, and we got our hams that day, too.

"Christmas started for Mr. Robins early enough that he had all his gag gifts lined up," explained Marshall. "One of the first ones was when the first part of Cummings was built and we had been over on Ellen Road just jumbled all up together. Well, that long hallway just looked like a race track to us. So, jokingly, we asked for motorscooters so we could get to the bathroom. We didn't get motorscooters, but the secretaries all got fur-lined pots just in case we didn't make it.

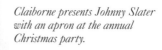

Claiborne presents Johnny Slater with an apron at the annual Christmas party.

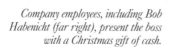

Company employees, including Bob Habenicht (far right), present the boss with a Christmas gift of cash.

"World's Best Boss"

"Our receptionist was so cold-natured," said Marshall, "that she shivered all winter long, so she got a pair of long johns with sequins and lace. The gifts he would give were very meaningful and funny to those that received them.

"At Thanksgiving every new employee was told automatically (by some of the veteran employees) that the turkeys were live," said Marshall, "that you had to go out in the warehouse and catch your own. Depending upon how gullible you were, you know you were terrified the week before how you were gonna get this turkey home. Somebody would usually go the day the turkeys arrived, go back to the warehouse, and come back with a bandaged finger."

Another Robins employee, Georgette Tignor, who started with the company in 1951, recalled the annual awards presentations made by Claiborne.

"Mr. Robins would come down personally and hand out the five-year and ten-year awards. I don't remember which award it was, the five or ten, but he would save me for last every time, and I knew what was coming. And I was always puckering up for kisses or something. I was sitting behind him and had blacked out my four front teeth ... people were in hysterics because he didn't see me. He finally turned around and looked. One time he kissed me on waxed lips — silly stuff like that. We were so small we were a family, always doing things like that."

"When I got married," said Marshall, "Mr. and Mrs. Robins gave me a mixer, so at Christmas I was going to make him a fruitcake, which I did, and the recipe was for a big cake, so I decided to divide it into three pans. I gave it to him, he thanked me, and never said a word.

"About two months later, I cut my own fruitcake and it was so hard you couldn't get a knife through it. And he was just as gracious about that fruitcake that they couldn't possibly have eaten or even gotten cut, as he would have been if I had cooked this magnificent thing.

"We always celebrated his birthday in the lunchroom," Marshall explained, "and one year with my new mixer I made him a cake, and each layer was about one inch tall. And I brought it in and he acted like it was the nicest birthday cake he had ever had, and it was three small pancakes. I wasn't all that great a cook, but we truly were, when we were small, a family."

Claiborne's feelings for his employees began to show in many ways as the company surged forward, such as offering free coffee in the lunchroom for all employees.

"Someone asked me once how much that cost," said Claiborne, chuckling. "I told them that I didn't have the slightest idea. I said I could call down to accounting and find out, but I never have, because if I did I'd probably cancel it.

"We did things like that because we thought it was a good business investment. We thought that if we had to defend it, we could justify it. We gave employees a small check on their birthdays, but it was the fact that we recognized the employee that was important."

Claiborne's largess grew with the company's success. A Robins tradition was born when he left his office one day in 1952 and made his way back into the plant for his weekly routine of keeping in touch with his employees. He stopped in the packaging, manufacturing and shipping departments to deliver a cheery word and a smile. He wanted the employees to see the president of the company, and he made a point of it, as Georgette Tignor recalled.

"He came down to see us — he had more time then — he used to come down and walk through and everybody was the same — office, plant, maintenance — everyone was treated the same. He was always joking. He knew everyone's name."

One time when he was visiting the packaging area, Claiborne mentioned that he was planning to go to New York. One of the women said that she had never been to New York, and Claiborne turned to the next woman in the line and asked her if she had

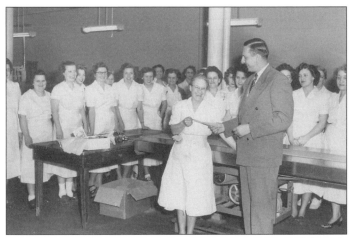

Claiborne with "Miss Teeny," Alma May Robertson, and the women of the packaging department in the 1940s.

been to New York. "No," she said. He went down the line asking the same question, and only one woman had been to New York, but she had only changed trains in Pennsylvania Station. Of the 30 women on the line only one had been to New York.

"Well, I'm going to see to it that you go," Claiborne said, pledging to sponsor the trip within 90 days. The first of the Robins company trips was born.

The Robins employees left early on a Friday morning by train, arriving in New York City at about 2:00 in the afternoon. The employees each had $100 spending money, a gift from the company, and tour guides took them to the Statue of Liberty, the Battery, the Empire State Building, and to many attractions of the city in which Claiborne had lived for a summer as a young man.

"We bought out the Latin Quarter nightclub that night, and we had the whole place to ourselves, just about," said Claiborne. "It was a special performance for us. The next night we took them to dinner at the Rainbow Room, on top of the RCA building. They got the best in nightclubbing and food and view, etc. Then we brought them back on Sunday afternoon and got back at 9:30 or 10 p.m. It was such a success that we estimated that the roughly

The company enjoys a visit to the Empire State Building and the Broadway show, "South Pacific," while on their trip to New York City in 1953.

$200 we spent per person was paid back within a few weeks by the increased production."

"I was fortunate enough to be one who got all four trips," remembered long-time Robins employee Johnny Gordon, "and you really would have to be there to appreciate how great they were. The first two were to New York, and for many of us it was our first trip to New York. I remember we were at the Rainbow Room, which was the ultimate, and then the Latin Quarter, a very famous nightclub. Mr. Robins liked nightclubs, he really did. We got to see the Rockettes, as well as trips to China Town, and I remember we went to the Statue of Liberty. We also got to see "South Pacific" with Mary Martin. Well, she was pretty much the rage then, so it was a real treat."

Fair to all his employees, Claiborne compensated those unable to attend company trips, as Robins employee Georgette Tignor recalled. "He gave the equivalent in a bonus-type arrangement of what he figured the cost per employee would be to go on those trips. He was always fair."

"World's Best Boss," was the caption under a Miami Herald newspaper photo of Claiborne and two employees splashing in the Miami Beach surf November 18, 1954. More than 100 of his employees had piled on a train and partied down the coast to Miami, where they were guests of the A. H. Robins Company at the Versailles Hotel. As before, the company gave each employee $100 spending money for a four-day trip, all expenses paid. No one enjoyed it more than Claiborne.

"One of my favorite things," recalled Marshall Phillips, "was

Top photo, Claiborne receives the key to Miami Beach. Front row, left to right: Bernice Bryant, Irene Wright, the mayor of Miami Beach, Claiborne, Joe Cordle and Dave Mefford. Behind Claiborne, left to right: Rose Scott Windsor, Vangie Windsor and Burwell Robinson. Bottom photo, poolside at the Versailles Hotel, with Lora and Claiborne in the foreground.

Lora, Claiborne and Marshall Phillips, foreground, enjoy the Miami surf. Group includes, left to right: front row, Johnny Gordon, Bernice Bryant, Dot Oakley, Louise Green, George Ashford; middle row, Carlton Gammon, Shorty Bolts, Grayson Kirtland, Al Kenney, Rose Scott Windsor, Irene Wright, Joyce Windsor Eacho; back row, Tony Steinbrecker, Johnny Slater, Dave Mefford, Mal Freeman, Thelma Messer.

when Mr. Robins and one of the other secretaries and myself, we had a picture taken running in the surf and it came out in the same magazine that Marilyn Monroe came out in. That's my one claim to fame. This was a little magazine called *Focus*, I believe. Marilyn Monroe was on one page and Mr. Robins and Kathy Britton and I were on the other."

Claiborne had not planned anything special to celebrate his 20th anniversary at the company, but his employees had something in mind for April 9, 1956. Claiborne was suspicious on that spring morning when the home office employees did not take their coffee break, and when Lora came into his office he knew a surprise was in the making.

Claiborne was ushered down to the lunchroom where all his employees were assembled. Dr. Eugene Jackson, medical director and senior vice president, was the master of ceremonies. He asked Gertrude Winston, a current employee who had the longest service at A. H. Robins Company, to make a presentation.

"WORLD'S BEST BOSS"

There was a check for $4,200 and a scroll that read: "Presented to E. Claiborne Robins with gratitude and affection on the occasion of his 20th anniversary as president by all personnel of A. H. Robins Company, Inc., A. H. Robins Inter-American Corporation, and the A. H. Robins Company of Canada, Ltd." The employees had turned the tables. They had pooled their money to send Claiborne and Lora on the vacation of their choice.

Claiborne and Lora receive a $4200 check from their employees for a vacation. At left is Dr. Eugene Jackson. At right is Gertrude Winston.

Claiborne and Lora decided on Acapulco, and the trip was scheduled for the coming winter. Lora and Claiborne were to catch a 7:30 a.m. plane from Byrd Field in Richmond to New York, and then on to Mexico.

On the morning of their departure, the couple woke to some of the worst weather of the winter, and as they made their way to the airport their car slipped and slid on ice an inch thick. They made it to the airport, but 30 minutes late. Eastern Airlines had held the plane because there were a 100+ A. H. Robins employees who had fought the weather to see the boss off. "It was quite a touching experience," Claiborne remembered.

Claiborne and Lora enjoyed the beaches and entertainment. A highlight of their trip, however, was a day out in the Pacific trolling for sailfish.

Company employees gather at Byrd Field to send Claiborne and Lora off to Acapulco.

Left, Claiborne lands his sailfish, then Lora lands her sailfish. Right, Claiborne and Lora posing with their catch in Acapulco in 1956.

Claiborne caught a large one. He battled 45 minutes to land the 150-pound fish, sticking to the fishing code that required him to battle the fish alone, with no help from the crew. "It was strenuous" he said. "When you catch one you don't want another right away." Then Lora caught one, and since it was a bit larger than Claiborne's, they had her fish mounted and sent back to Richmond as a trophy.

The Robinses so enjoyed the beaches of Acapulco that Claiborne was prompted to plan another company trip to a tropical destination: Cuba. Claiborne loved Havana, which in pre-Castro days was a delightful vacation city, with gambling and bargain shopping. So in 1957 the A. H. Robins Company took 132 employees on a five-day trip to Cuba.

"*LIFE* magazine called and said they wanted to come along on the trip," remembered Claiborne. "We were a bit uncertain, and they said they would come anyway. So we said come on, with some misgivings, but 20 years later doctors were still asking where we were going to take our employees that year," Claiborne said.

They boarded a special train in Richmond and flew from Miami to Havana. Including the $100 spending money Claiborne provided his employees, the trip cost the company $40,000. Claiborne and Lora joined the crowd in the hotel pool, sightseeing around the city, and dancing the mambo in the nightclubs. Wearing sombreros and carrying bottles of rum, they returned to Richmond by train from Miami in high spirits.

"The really ultimate trip was Havana," said Johnny Gordon, "because for many people it was their first airplane flight. Mr. and Mrs. Robins were just everywhere, and saw that every individual had a great time.

"We were warned that we were going to have a *LIFE* reporter and *LIFE* photographer, and they were kind of like '60 Minutes' in those days," recalled Gordon. "If there was any dirt, they were

Claiborne takes the company to Havana, Cuba, in 1957. Pictured behind Claiborne is Gariella Campos and Al Kenney (with hat).

going to dig it up and put it out. We were all a little nervous about having the two of them, but the photographer was a young man and the reporter was a young girl. Before we got to Petersburg they were having as good a time as anybody, and they had a ball the entire trip.

"We got nothing but super publicity on that, but we were afraid they were gonna cramp our style. It turned out they were just one of us, and they really did enjoy it. At beach time, Mr. and Mrs. Robins were right there with us, and if they didn't enjoy it they sure did put on a good act. They were just part of the crowd,

Havana, Cuba, 1957
Clockwise, from top:
Pan American Airlines welcomes the company to Cuba; Mary Weinstock, third from left, samples Cuban libations with her companions; Claiborne on the shoulders of John Richman and Dr. Robert Murphey; Lora with mariachi band; employees enjoy Cuban cigars.

Photo: Paul Schutzer, LIFE Magazine, © Time Inc.

Clockwise, from top: Claiborne and Lora poolside at the Hotel Nacional de Cuba; partying on the train home, Henry Barnette sits on Pop McKim's shoulders; Claiborne receives a thank you kiss on the train from Miami to Richmond; Lora, left, under the Robins company sign in Havana.

and they didn't inhibit people, but I think everybody respected the standards of Mr. and Mrs. Robins, and we never had to worry about people misbehaving."

The Havana trip was just a few months before Castro came to power, but the group had no sense of unrest. On the company trip, however, Claiborne noticed that Cuban President Batista had assigned some guards to protect them while they were there, protection against the growing threat posed by the insurgent Fidel Castro.

Back in Richmond the following week, a quarter would buy the December 16 issue of *LIFE* magazine with the Robins trip on page 125. With seven photos of Robins employees swimming, nightclubbing, sightseeing, and dancing on the train ride back to Richmond, the trip was well covered by the national magazine.

Washington D.C. was the destination for 340 A. H. Robins employees on October 24, 1958. On this trip employees boarded a train at Richmond's Broad Street Station at 5 p.m. and had the choice of turkey or seafood as they dined during the two-hour trip to Union Station in the nation's capital.

From there they were bussed to the Shubert Theater, where they saw actress Tallulah Bankhead in "Crazy October," a farce about life in a West Virginia roadhouse. After the play, the Robins

Claiborne aboard the train to Washington D.C., October 24, 1958. Above, with Pete and Georgette Tignor (center and far right).

Lora and Claiborne with Tallulah Bankhead at the performance of "Crazy October" in Washington D.C. on October 24, 1958.

special train took them back to Richmond.

Employees filled the seats and lined the walls of the lunchroom on July 7, 1959, hoping to hear the destination of the next company trip. Claiborne obviously enjoyed the occasion, striding into the lunchroom with his big grin.

"This meeting is to tell you about your next trip," he said, and the applause thundered across the room. He teased them with little bits of information, but did not mention the destination. "It's going to be next May," he said. Finally, he told them where: "We're going to fly non-stop to Los Angeles, stay there for two nights, and then to Las Vegas for two nights."

Yet this trip was not to be. Senator Estes Kefauver of Tennessee was heading a committee investigating drug prices and practices within the pharmaceutical industry, and the senator was attracting national attention.

Reluctantly, Claiborne decided that the trip would fuel the notion that pharmaceutical companies were earning excessive profits and wasting money on frivolous activities. Making the trip more prohibitive still, the Internal Revenue Service gave notice

Claiborne and his employees gather together in the lunchroom.

that the trips could be taxed as income to the employees.

Claiborne canceled the trip, but gave employee bonuses to soften the disappointment. It was the end of a fabulous tradition, but the company would enjoy its reputation as a firm generous to its employees, not only because of the company trips, but because of the close and personal relationship that employees had with their boss.

"People like to be recognized, and we made every effort that we could to recognize people," explained Claiborne. "I used to call up people when they had their five-year, ten-year, 15- and 20-year anniversaries and just say, 'I just wanted you to know that I haven't forgotten. Today is the day!'

"I felt close to a number of our employees, of course Mal Freeman and his wife," said Claiborne. "There were a number of other employees that I felt reasonably close to, but I don't know that you could determine that — there's a fine point — you don't want to get too close because then your judgment might get clouded a little bit."

Claiborne's generosity and his personal attention to his employees paid off in loyalty and increased production. Johnny

Gordon, who came to work at A. H. Robins from the University of Richmond in 1949, expressed the attitude of his co-workers.

"I was so tied up in A. H. Robins that it was just a way of life. There was just no job that Mr. Robins or Ted Heffner could ask you to do that you wouldn't do regardless of what was required. They were never demanding, there was just something about the two that required you to do your very best."

"We were reputed to have the best sales force in the entire pharmaceutical industry," said Claiborne. "I'm not foolish enough to think that we were just so smart in picking; I don't believe that was the entire story. I believe that maybe we picked some ordinary salesmen and made them into better ones."

With his civility and warmth, Claiborne even won over those employees who failed to make the grade at Robins and who had to be fired. "One of the hardest things to do is let somebody go," said Claiborne, "and I had that task, unfortunately, on a few occasions. One person said they had never been let go and made to feel so good. I always took the approach that they had many qualities that we admired and that they had a lot of things which could make them successful in other fields, but that they just didn't seem to be able to fit in our situation.

"I felt we had to let them go, but I urged them not to give up hope because they do have good qualities which would enable them possibly to succeed in other fields. And when we could, we tried to help them if they were worthy of helping."

Recognized by his employees as a caring boss, Claiborne was also recognized among his industry peers, and he received numerous honors for his civic and industry efforts. One honor, which is particularly important to Claiborne, was given to him in 1966 by the American Newcomen Society of North America, a prestigious organization that recognizes successful business leaders at an international level.

Virginia Governor Mills E. Godwin Jr., himself a member of the Newcomen Society, introduced Claiborne at a dinner in

Richmond on May 19. Claiborne told the story of the A. H. Robins Company, and in his concluding remarks he stated his philosophy concerning his employees:

"We hear a lot about morale, but few recognize that the basic principles of morale involve only that good, old-time philosophy of the golden rule. When you are good to people, usually they are good to you — and that, in my book, is the foundation for a good employer/employee relationship."

Claiborne promoted from within the organization, which met with mixed results. "It is absolutely true that a good salesman may not be a good manager, and vice versa," he acknowledged. "We tried to find men who had demonstrated drive and the desire to succeed, and who had a reputation for being hard workers. Hard work is probably the key to success."

Luck sometimes put his best men on the sales force. "We had a fellow, an older gentleman, maybe 60, who worked Texas, down around San Antonio," said Claiborne. "He was not a great salesman, and he called on the doctors not even knowing much about his product. He presented the product, what it had in it, and asked the doctor to write it.

"It was kind of old-fashioned, but something about him appealed to the doctors and he did very, very well. Another salesman, this one in Richmond, just went into the doctor's office, left a sample, and told him he was counting on them to write it. He got a lot of business."

Claiborne extended his hospitality by hosting a dinner at his home, Clear View, for his salesmen and other employees. At most sales meetings and on other occasions he and Lora entertained salesmen who were charmed to be guests in their home. Claiborne gave Lora the credit for this successful effort and was grateful for her ability to entertain almost every A. H. Robins employee, including a 500-man sales force.

"If you plan your work, it's easy," said Lora. "Everything was cooked that day. We had shrimp Creole by request, year after year

Lora, right, hosting one of the many parties held at Clear View.

after year. I had started making batter bread, and one man said he didn't want anything else except batter bread!" she laughed.

The menu also included cherry-topped cheesecake and ham biscuits. She remembered having 96 people for dinner one Christmas when Claiborne increased the number of guests without telling her. "They were all over the house, sitting on the steps and everywhere else, but it was great fun," said Lora.

Lora did most of the work herself, with only their house-keeper, Martha Scott, and an occasional helper in the kitchen. In later years Claiborne persuaded her to use a caterer because of the enormous amount of work involved with having the large buffet parties.

The dinners were always successful, and they received many letters of gratitude from salesmen brimming over with appreciation for the opportunity to visit the president's home. "If they only knew how much fun we got out of it," Lora said.

Lora believed as intensely as Claiborne that a strong personal relationship between the sales force and the company was important. "I think it was most effective," she said, "because many of the men we entertained said they had never even seen the chief executive [of their previous employer], much less been entertained by him."

Claiborne also knew the value of entertaining employees. "It was important because the salesmen felt a personal loyalty to the company," he explained, "they felt that they knew everybody, right up to the top."

On the day of Claiborne's 50-year anniversary with A. H. Robins on November 1, 1983, Claiborne knew something unusual was coming up.

"One of the big surprises that I had was when employees gave a big party for me on my 50th year with Robins," remembered Claiborne. "More than a thousand employees .... They kept it a secret and told me they wanted me to go outside — they had something they wanted me to see. When I went outside — it was in the side parking lot — about a thousand people had gathered.

"They not only presented me with a beautiful array of rare coins from each of the countries that we did business in, and had it all framed and so forth, they asked me to look over across the highway, and there was a big billboard that had been put up, and the billboard said — it had a picture of me," he chuckled, "'THANK YOU FOR 50 YEARS OF LEADERSHIP, MR. ROBINS, FROM 5,600 FELLOW A. H. ROBINS EMPLOYEES.' And it was such a complete surprise. Nobody had even dropped a hint."

Claiborne was presented with the collection of gold coins from 14 of the countries in which A. H. Robins had company facilities. The coins were mounted in a double glass frame for viewing from both sides. The retired president was visibly moved, and his response centered on a dominant theme of his leadership, that employees are the most important asset of any company.

Claiborne termed his 50-year career exciting, "but more exciting than that," he added, "has been my privilege to be associated with the finest group of people in this whole wide world. You and I know, and I know especially, that what has been accomplished would not have been possible without the all-out support and enthusiastic cooperation of all of you here today, and all of our other people in this country and throughout the world.

Thirty-nine-year veteran employee Vangie Windsor presents Claiborne with a collection of gold coins on the occasion of his 50th anniversary with the company in 1983. Photo: © Don Eiler, Richmond, Virginia.

We have been blessed with so many things, but particularly we have been blessed with our people. I want to thank you for all that you have done to make this company what it is today."

Executive Vice President Robert G. Watts presided over the ceremonies, and spoke for the employees: "You have been an outstanding leader for us, you have recognized people, you have treated people kindly, you have treated them lovingly and with great respect. And there is not one of us standing here today who does not have thoughts going through his mind relating to all that. It is with these special thoughts in mind that we wanted to pay tribute to you and to salute you today."

Earlier, Claiborne Jr. had paid a similar tribute to his father in an address to the 20th stockholders meeting in May of 1983, when Claiborne was also honored for 50 years of company leadership.

"I hope you will join me in saluting the man who put this company on the road to success," said Claiborne, Jr. "He is a man who has provided dynamic leadership, a man who is a proven manager and motivator, and a man who has demonstrated how good people, good products and hard work can bring great results. He has indeed been a leader of our company, our industry and our community for 50 years, and we salute him today as we shall at other times throughout this year. A friend to all of our people, and an inspiration as well, he is our chairman and my father, E. Claiborne Robins." The applause was thunderous.

VIII

THE PATRIARCH

The lives of community leaders are often thinly stretched between the demands of business, family and civic organizations. As one of Richmond's budding leaders, Claiborne was deeply involved in all three.

During the 1950s, business and civic matters began to compete with family responsibilities as Claiborne filled the role of chief executive and undertook a personal commitment to his community. As a result, Claiborne had to rely on Lora for family matters.

"I'm afraid she had most of the responsibility for raising the children," said Claiborne. "But she was very understanding on that count and that has been a great help. Fortunately, I've been very lucky that my children turned out pretty well. They haven't had any serious problems, and in these days and times you are very grateful for that."

Claiborne's civic duties began when the children were still young. In 1952 they included the presidency of the Richmond Chamber of Commerce and the boards of the University of Richmond and Central National Bank. The year before, he had been president of the Medical College of Virginia Alumni Association.

Claiborne was also a faithful member of Rotary Club, and was renowned for having attended weekly meetings most of his adult life. Even while traveling, Claiborne was loyal to Rotary, and he attended meetings in many foreign countries.

Claiborne in the 1950s.

As A. H. Robins expanded, Claiborne's civic duties covered a broad range of interests that went well beyond meetings and boardrooms. In 1955, he was able to satisfy a lifelong love of sports when he helped save Richmond's minor league baseball club.

Claiborne, Fritz Sitterding, Richard Reynolds, Dan Friedman, Milton Markel, and Jack Bernstein bought the Richmond Virginians, the farm team of the New York Yankees. They did so because of a love of baseball and for the benefit of the city.

"It was a very harmonious and pleasant relationship. It was a civic undertaking," Claiborne recalled. "I don't know how the five of us got together. We knew we were all interested in baseball, so I spent many a night in April and early May when you would have maybe 500 people in the stands and you'd wonder why 500 even came because of the drizzly weather. While Richmond is a fairly good baseball town, it is a notoriously poor sports town, as towns go.

"We owned the club for three years," said Claiborne. "One year we made a little bit of money, two years we lost money, because owning a minor league club is no way to make money. We had a working arrangement with the New York Yankees.

"Of course, as always is the case, just when you get going good and somebody does well, they call up the best player you've got, and even though you have a good team for part of the year, usually you end up at the end of the year with their having pulled out three or four of the best. So it's pretty tough to win play-offs. We did get into the play-offs one time, and that was the year we made a little bit of money.

"Finally, the Yankees came to us and said, 'We'd like to buy you out. What do you want for the club?' We all got together and we decided we wanted exactly, to the penny, what we had in it. We didn't want any profit, we just wanted the money that we had lost and what we put into it.

"And so the Yankees agreed to that, and we sold the club, and we broke even, to the penny. We gave a little party that night. I'm sure it's the only party that's ever been given anywhere to celebrate breaking even," he chuckled.

"It was a very congenial group. It was a very heterogeneous group. I mean, Milton Markel and Dan Friedman were Jewish, and Fritz Sitterding, I reckon, is Irish Catholic, and Richard Reynolds, I don't know what he was. We never had a discordant note. Those five got along swimmingly together, and we usually agreed on things."

Claiborne was president of the club when the Yankees won the World Series in 1956, and he attended a World Series game to see Yankee stars Mickey Mantle, Roger Maris, Yogi Berra and others. His memory of the Yankees, however, was later tainted.

"I had one experience with the lack of caring of the Yankees," he remembered. "We alternated the presidency, and I happened to be president of the Richmond club the year the Yankees won the World Series. I thought, oh boy, being the president of the Richmond club, I'll get a ticket to the World Series. After all, we were a farm club of the Yankees.

"I managed to get a ticket, so I went up to New York, to Yankee Stadium, and in the old Yankee stadium there were two huge posts, and if you had a ticket behind one of those posts you couldn't see anything except the right field and the center fielder. That was about it. So guess what they gave me? One of those tickets behind the post.

"Well, I was furious, of course, so I went down to the Yankee ticket office and protested violently, and by the time I got to somebody who had the position to do anything, it was the third inning. They gave me a nice ticket down at home plate, so I saw about six innings of the game from the good seat. But they gave me the only seat they couldn't sell, so that gave me a pretty good indication of how caring the Yankees were. They were a cold-blooded organization. They were efficient, but cold."

One spring, the Yankees played an exhibition game with the Richmond Virginians, and Lora and Claiborne gave a party for

Casey Stengel, legendary manager of the Yankees, and other Yankee executives.

"The Yankees were playing an exhibition game in Richmond," recalled Claiborne. "Casey Stengel was the manager. We decided we'd give a party for Casey and two or three of the Yankee brass who were in town for the game. We invited just a close few friends. Among those present were Tom Cockrell, a great baseball fan, and a few other friends who were baseball fans, a relatively small party.

"We sent word to Casey that we'd pick him up at the hotel — the John Marshall — and so at 5:30 I was there and introduced myself as Claiborne Robins, and he got in the car, and we went on out to Clear View, and we got to chatting and so forth, and I soon got the direct impression that he didn't have the slightest idea who I was.

"He was a great manager, but he was scatter-brained and, of course, he talked so much that he didn't give anybody else time. He was so busy talking that I didn't get time to get a word in edgewise, which was all right because he was fascinating. But as we went along, he had no idea who I was, and so we rolled up to the gate and started into Clear View, and he looked up and said, 'Geez, this guy must be really in the dough,'" chuckled Claiborne.

"Well, when you have a party, Casey was the man to have. He was full of stories, baseball stories, and he had everybody in that place around him. And he just kept everybody enthralled for a couple hours. Casey had enough to drink that he didn't stop talking from the time he got there, and nobody cared.

"Tom Cockrell took him home and said it was the highlight of his life. To this very day — 'til he died — I don't think Casey ever had the slightest idea who his host was, or who I was. It didn't seem to matter. He thought I was a driver that had been sent down to pick him up. I guess it never occurred to him that I'd come myself."

Claiborne's interest in baseball was passed on to his children who remember seeing the Richmond Colts baseball team play at old Moore's Field. Later, he took the family to the International League games. Going to Parker Field when the Virginians were in town became a family routine. The family custom was to buy a score book, so the children could join in scoring the games.

"He observed that it didn't help his enjoyment of the game to have bought the team," recalled Claiborne's daughter, Betty, "especially when the batter at the plate would hit several successive foul balls into the stands at $5 a shot."

Claiborne had another habit. If the Virginians were leading late in the game he would herd the family into the car and go home. "If they lose it now, I don't want to see it," he told Lora and the children.

Claiborne Jr. became so enamored with baseball that he held a dream throughout his childhood to play professional ball. His father, however, tried to discourage his ambition.

"Son, there's more money in the pharmaceutical business than there is in baseball," he pointed out. He had patience with Claiborne Jr.'s early devotion to a professional athletic career, believing that the boy would out-grow that ambition.

As a diversion from baseball, Claiborne saw to it that his son learned the family business. The boy worked in the mail room, ran a fork-lift, and did other jobs for the company during summer vacations, later detailing doctors in the Virginia Beach area.

"Betty and Ann Carol never did express any great interest in getting involved, so I didn't insist that they do," said Claiborne of his daughters' role in A. H. Robins

Claiborne and Claiborne Jr. on the day of his graduation from 8th grade in 1957.

Company. "Of course, they used to kid me a little bit about not having any females heading the company."

Betty had also worked for the company filing and packaging, but realized that the world of business seemed relegated to men. "I didn't sense a difference then, but now, of course, I am aware that his expectations for his daughters were quite different than they were for his son," she said. "I don't remember him ever suggesting to me that I think about a career, but then that was typical of the times."

Claiborne, Jr. inherited not only his father's love for baseball, but also learned to play golf with his father. "I'd go out with Dad and play nine holes, because that's all Dad usually played," said Claiborne Jr. "I used to joke that for a number of years I thought golf was a nine-hole game."

Claiborne was a nine-hole golfer, even on the occasions when he played with business associates. In the '50s and '60s Robins sponsored golf tournaments for its executives as another way to inspire loyalty. As company president, Claiborne would get the tournament off to a good start, then disappear after nine holes so he could go back to work.

Basketball was also a favorite family pastime, as Betty recalled. "In the mid-'50s the Richmond Spiders had a top-notch basketball team. We attended every game and entertained the players at the house. They had a center named Bob Witt and a guard named Warren Mills, and I still remember the excitement of those games."

While sports remained one of Claiborne's closest interests, his involvement with the pharmaceutical industry always took precedence. Honoring his commitment to civic involvement, Claiborne desired to recognize pharmacists within their communities. During the 1950s, this gave rise to the Bowl of Hygeia Award, which was initiated by Claiborne. The Bowl of Hygeia is the Greek symbol of medicine and the award became the pharmaceutical industry's most enduring honor.

"I was very aware when I got out of pharmacy school how few

pharmacists were actively involved in their communities," explained Claiborne. "I thought about it for some time, but we did not have enough capital to do anything about it until 1958.

"The Bowl of Hygeia is the internationally recognized symbol of pharmacy, so we asked the pharmacy association of each state to have their members select the pharmacist in that state who had made the greatest contribution to their state and nation.

"We finally got a nominee from all the states, Puerto Rico, the District of Columbia, and all the provinces of Canada. We brought the candidate and his spouse to Richmond for several days, recognized them at a big banquet, and usually the Governor of Virginia welcomed them. We took them sightseeing to Williamsburg, Yorktown, and Richmond, of course."

Each of the candidates received the Bowl of Hygeia award, which was polished mahogany with a gold plaque. Robins also arranged for *Time* magazine to make up a *Time* cover with each recipient's photo. The framed cover was a memento the pharmacist could hang in his shop. The added value of the publicity and good-will for the A. H. Robins Company made it a prudent business investment that continued to pay off for 30 years.

"There are about 20 awards, but the Bowl of Hygeia award was the first in pharmacy," explained Claiborne. "It got local coverage in newspapers and national coverage in the pharmacy journals. I believe it to be the highest award in pharmacy today," Claiborne said. "I think that the fact that I received the honorary presidency of the American Pharmaceutical Association for 1992 is attributable to my having established the Bowl of Hygeia award."

With his warm smile and solid credentials, Claiborne became one of the best spokesmen for the pharmaceutical industry, and he was elected by his peers to the chairmanship of the Pharmaceutical Manufacturers Association for 1968. His already overloaded schedule had to be manipulated to squeeze in meetings across the nation as he struggled to clarify to the public the benefits and the value of the industry he represented.

At the time, Congress was scrutinizing the healthy profits made by drug companies, and the man on the street saw the cost of many prescriptions jump. Claiborne told audiences across the country that profits were needed to support increasingly expensive research and development of new drugs. While some drugs were more expensive at the pharmacy, he pointed out, people were living healthier lives, with life expectancy decades longer than when he was a boy. His message was emphasized by the pharmaceutical industry for many years, and the tall man with the wide smile and obvious sincerity made many friends for the industry that year.

"I've been fortunate to receive the highest rewards," acknowledged Claiborne. "I've won the highest award from the wholesalers. I've won the highest award from the American Pharmaceutical Association. In fact, I was recently honored by being the honorary president. That's from all the pharmacists in the country. It is a great tribute to the admiration that the pharmacists have for the company, too."

Despite the many demands outside his family, Claiborne spent time with the children when he could, and often they went for a Sunday ride around town.

"I remember long Sunday drives with the whole family spent exploring new areas of a growing Richmond," said Betty, "and ending up usually at the Howard Johnson's on the north side for ice cream cones. I remember Buddy, the poodle, being fed his own ice cream cone by Mother."

Sometimes they drove around the Byrd Park Lake area, where Martha Taylor Robins and Claiborne had lived when he was a boy.

"On very hot summers, pre-air-conditioning, we would escape in the evenings with a ride in the car around Byrd Park Lake to watch the fountain in the center change colors," recalled Betty. Ann Carol remembered driving through downtown Richmond to look at the windows of Miller & Rhoads and Thalhimer's department stores.

Lora and Claiborne at home at Clear View.

Claiborne Jr. remembered other outings. "Dad was involved with the Richmond Chamber of Commerce and took us to the grand opening of the Sealtest Ice Cream plant in Scott's Addition, just off of the boulevard," said Claiborne Jr. "About 6:00 that night he took the whole family down to tour the new plant. I remember that like it was yesterday. The thing that particularly sticks with me is that we walked through the freezer. It was just something neat that we did."

The family usually went out to dinner on Saturday nights, often to Byrams, a favorite restaurant on Broad Street. "They had a love for fine restaurants," said Betty, "whether going to Byrams for dinner or to a gourmet restaurant on a trip."

Hot summer evenings in the south were often spent cruising the town in the American automobile. Claiborne recalled the "wheels" he enjoyed over the years. He owned a Pontiac after World War II, and the family dubbed the car "The Green Hornet." "It was a tough car and served us well for several years," Claiborne said.

He thought a convertible would be fun and owned one in the 1950s for a short time. However, he soon found he did not like it as much as he had thought he would. "Too hot in the summer and too cold in the winter," was his assessment.

As the family prospered, Claiborne moved up to a Cadillac and liked the big, comfortable car. Feeling strongly about supporting American car companies — while regularly protesting his children's and grandchildren's choices of foreign automobiles — Claiborne has continued to buy Cadillacs for the past 40 years trading them in every two or three years.

The family's new-found status was not appreciated by all the children, however, as Betty described her own adjustment. "I felt a growing sense of discomfort at being 'different' in the amount of wealth we seemed to have. Mother, unsympathetic to my need not to stand out, ignored my strong-felt feelings that she not come to pick me up in our Cadillac, and I remember when I saw one day that she had come despite my request, I remember walking quickly away where she didn't spot me and going to the bus stop to take my usual mode of transportation home."

While he was careful that his children remained unspoiled, he was generous with them. When Betty expressed reluctance for a debutante party, Claiborne and Lora coaxed her by hiring the Glenn Miller Band. The band which played the swing jazz that Claiborne and Lora loved, performed for the A. H. Robins employees the following night and again, several years later, for Ann Carol's debutante party.

"Money was always available to us, usually through Mother, who dealt with us for our day-to-day needs," said Betty. "He did buy a car for all of us on our 16th birthday. I did not know, however, until I left home about the trusts that had been set up for me by him and by Grandmother Robins."

Martha Taylor Robins had bestowed her stock holdings to her grandchildren, again showing the generosity that was one of her strongest traits. Her sacrifices and frugal living had not only supported Claiborne in his youth, but would furnish rewards to her grandchildren.

While the grandchildren were still quite young, however, the physical condition of Claiborne's mother had begun to deteriorate. Her mental faculties were failing, and she had become senile in her old age. Martha had been living in a nursing home, where Claiborne visited regularly, and one visit in particular struck a vivid memory for Betty.

"Grandmother was in the nursing home and was unable to recognize even my father. I remember my sadness on that day when I went with him. He brought her the radio he had bought, the only thing he said that the nurses had indicated seemed to give her pleasure. I stayed in the car, and when he came out with the radio still in hand and said that the nurses had already gotten her one, I could have cried."

It was a deeply felt loss to the family and her friends

Martha Taylor Robins on a trip to Florida in 1945.

when Martha Taylor Robins died September 22, 1957, just four days after her 74th birthday. Mother and son had grown close over the years, having cemented a bond of love and mutual respect. Claiborne had depended upon his mother as his sole parent ever since the death of his father, when Claiborne was only two years old.

Martha had struggled through a long life of hardship and sacrifice, but she managed to shape Claiborne's personality by giving him solid values to live by, educating him, and bringing him into the family business. She was paid a tribute in the September 1957 issue of the "Robins Reader," which said, Mrs. Robins "was loved not only by all the workers, but by everyone she came in contact with. One knew immediately upon meeting her that she was friendly, kind and good."

Martha Taylor Robins, who had been a strong foundation for the A. H. Robins company for decades, was buried September 24, 1957 in Riverview Cemetery in Richmond beside her husband, who had preceded her by 47 years.

With his mother gone, sharing time with his family became more important to Claiborne. In an effort to seek refuge from business and civic pressures, the family spent time at one place Claiborne felt truly relaxed: Virginia Beach. He had spent many days at Virginia Beach during his college years, and before that had enjoyed good times at Willoughby with Mal Freeman.

In the early 1950s the children learned to share the love of the beach and love of nature from Lora, and they grew to love the seashore as much as their parents did.

"We spent summer vacations at Ocean View," remembered Betty, "and later at Marshall's Resort at Virginia Beach, and finally, month-long rentals at the Cockrell's cottage at Virginia Beach. All three of us went surfing with Daddy in the waves."

"We used to go every weekend, leave on Thursday and come back Sunday," said Claiborne. "We found the way to battle the traffic was to leave on Sunday morning about 7:00, and that's a way to miss it. It's a beautiful place, right on the ocean front.

"We built the main house in 1963; we had wanted to buy the house next door and it was not available. But after we started building the house, the gentleman who owned it decided he was gonna put it on the market, so we grabbed it because it was an incredibly good price.

"Lora kind of oversaw the construction, keeping an eye out for the things that should have been done and those that should not have been done," said Claiborne. "As it turned out at the time, we got the guest house and the lot in-between for $75,000. That same piece of property today is — the land alone — valued at $600,000 and some, not counting the house on it.

Lora and Claiborne at the beach.

"Anyway, we lived over there in the guest house while the other house was being completed. We still have the guest house. I rent it out, mostly to former Robins employees. It's booked solid for the summer, right through to October.

"Of course, I never made any money on it because keeping up a beach place is horrendously expensive. There is never a time when you don't have to spend a fortune because salt air eats up everything, including aluminum and copper and steel, you name it."

Originally, their beach property had no sea wall, so they built one to protect the beach front house. The new beach house became a haven for Claiborne, and the long summer days and nights there were a welcome respite from his busy life.

"My wife is in a major repair program right now," Claiborne said in 1992. "We virtually gutted the house on the inside. Hopefully, we will get to enjoy it, a little bit anyway. I told my wife I was afraid with our life expectancy we'd have a cost of about a $100,000 a year for the rest of our lives, just on this project."

Another favorite vacation enjoyed by the family for many years was their annual spring trip to the Golden Gate Hotel at the north end of Miami Beach. Claiborne was immersed in his business and therefore was only able to come down for a long weekend during the two week stay, so the children traveled south with their mother.

"We had a private cottage and it was like you were in your own home with living room, kitchen, and so on," Claiborne said. "We always took the children down, they always enjoyed it. I put the dirty work on my wife," he said with a guilty twinkle. "She wanted to drive, so she would drive the children down and I'd fly down later,"

"We played games, puzzles, counting blue cars and the like," said Lora. "The children were good. I told them I couldn't drive if they misbehaved. I got so I could drive that 1019 miles in 19 hours. I was flying low."

"We had fun on those pre-interstate highway trips through the Carolinas," recalled Betty, "stopping for pecan pie in South Carolina, reading the Burma Shave signs. Mother had a lead foot when driving, and I was navigator, watching out for those areas marked 'speedtrap' on the Triptik, a custom route prepared by the AAA.

"Also I remember the time our Buick's cloth convertible top started coming apart on the trip down, thanks to the cat we had at the time using it as a scratching post. Mother just dug into her purse and came up with an assortment of safety and bobby pins that got us through to Miami without having to stop for a repair. This was a typical example of Mother's sense of adventure and resourcefulness that made her such a unique companion and helpmate to Daddy as he was building his business."

On one Florida trip, Claiborne took the family to the Latin Quarter in Miami, an experience he recalled as one of his most memorable. "Milton Berle was the featured attraction at the Latin Quarter. We didn't know if the children were too young — they were in their early teens, or a little younger. Berle was at his prime. I've never seen an audience laugh almost continuously for the hour and a half Berle was on the stage, and he was out of this world as an entertainer. The audience just roared. The children still talk about it."

There were other vacations, too. They went to Canada one year and visited Niagara Falls, where they rode the Maid of the Mist tour boat beneath the roaring falls. They traveled to New York City when Betty was 12 years of age and went to one of the world's most famous restaurants, the Rainbow Room. "Betty ordered a club sandwich and a cola. Even in the French restaurants she ordered plain food so she would stay well and see everything," said Lora.

Lora drove the three children to Waco one summer to visit her family. While there, the children saw a miniature poodle and fell in love with him. "All three of us went to Texas with Mother," said Betty, "and bought our first poodle, 'Buddy,' and returned home with him to an unsuspecting father." Needless to say, Buddy became Claiborne's faithful companion for many years.

On a later vacation, Claiborne took Lora and the children to the Crazy Horse in Paris, one of the world's great burlesque

Claiborne, Lora, Claiborne Jr. and Betty visit Lora's parents, Mr. and Mrs. McGlasson, in Waco, Texas, in the mid-1940s.

houses. "Looking back on it I'm kind of surprised that I did," he said, "but it didn't faze them. They seemed to appreciate the fact that we took them along."

Taking his children to a burlesque house was very much in character for Claiborne, and, according to Ann Carol, her father's unabashed sexuality contributed to a healthy view of life.

"I think that had a major influence on me, and I think it gave me the ability to relate to the opposite gender," she said. "He was relaxed about sex, that it was not something to be afraid of, because he was comfortable with it. He wasn't uptight about sex and nudity.

"He projected the message that it was normal and a natural part of life and something to be enjoyed and not dirty and secretive like so many other people of the time felt it was. He was not prudish, but relaxed with himself and his own body. I think it contributed to a healthy sexuality."

Affectionate with his family, Claiborne was the originator of the "Robins' pat," a warm and doting touch to those he loved. "He is physically demonstrative," said Ann Carol.

"He and Mother both were always affectionate with us," said Betty. "I remember lots of hugs and kisses."

Claiborne had only one regret in family travels, that the children grew up before they traveled west as a family. "We tried our best, but we made the mistake of waiting too long to get the kids to go with us on a trip West, like we took on our honeymoon," said Claiborne, "and to go to all the national parks, but we couldn't get them to go.

"We said, 'Why?', and they said, 'We've seen it on television.' That wasn't the real reason. The real reason was that they had boyfriends or girlfriends, and they didn't particularly want to leave. If we had tried to do that when they were eight, nine and ten, they might have gone, but we waited til they were 13, 14, and 15, a little bit too late, so we never did get them to go West."

When the girls were old enough to date, many young men were attracted to Clear View. Lora set the deadlines for Betty and Ann

Carol to be home. If they stayed at Clear View watching TV in the den, Claiborne was the one who came downstairs and announced: "All good things must come to an end, sweetie," as Ann Carol remembered with a laugh. She strongly insists, however, that her parents were more "strict" with her than they were with Betty.

While Clear View had been a wonderful place to raise their children and rest and relax from the day's labor, Claiborne and Lora began to think of moving. Closet space in the house was limited, and other signs of age began to plague the home. Yet they loved the house and loved the location, where the flowers and trees had been carefully nurtured by Lora and their gardeners, Mickey and Kenneth. Through the years it provided a beautiful setting.

"When we bought it we found that the builders had done everything on the outside to make it look perfect, but they cut corners on the inside," Claiborne said. "We had to add a septic tank and a larger hot water heater, and some things like that. But it was a nice house and a gorgeous location and we always loved being there."

They decided to stay and simply rebuild the home just a few feet to the rear of the old house. They lived in the old house while the new one was going up, which took nearly three years because they hired the best artisans in the area to work on it. They moved into the new home in January 1981.

At home, Claiborne was very structured in his daily routine. The children remember that he would walk in the house within five minutes of seven, get his newspaper and a gin and tonic, and sit down in his wing chair to relax and catch up with the news. "We knew that was his time to settle down from the hustle and bustle of the day and we were not to disturb him," said Claiborne Jr.

"All of us had a family dinner afterwards," remembered Betty, "in the 'breakfast room,' a small dining room adjacent to the kitchen. As a teenager, I remember it being prepared and served, usually by Martha. It was a time where we all were gathered in a

Claiborne, Lora, Betty, Claiborne Jr. and Ann Carol pose for a photo at the breakfast table in the late 1950s.

non-rushed atmosphere, as opposed to breakfast. Topics were general — no intellectual games or such — at dinner."

Claiborne went to work every Saturday and occasionally on Sunday, though not all day on every weekend. Most weekends he would go to work on Saturday at 10 a.m., after a haircut at the John Marshall Hotel barber shop. He returned home about 1:30 p.m. He relished weekends when the office was silent: no telephones, no meetings. On the other hand, he would often take off from work to attend a game or some other children's event.

When the children were young, Claiborne took them to Sunday church services and came home to have dinner. Ann Carol recalled that Claiborne always had a Bristol Cream before dinner. Betty said, "Mother prepared fried chicken for the midday meal at home every Sunday after Daddy would return from taking us to church."

After dinner, around 2 p.m., Claiborne would go to the office and come back at about 5 p.m. Generally, that was his schedule for 25 years.

Although Claiborne felt he didn't spend enough time with his children while they were growing up, he nonetheless managed to infuse his values into them.

"He exemplifies the golden rule," said Betty. "He instilled honesty and integrity in his children. I want to live up to his ideals."

"The shadow of my dad is always here, and I like it that way, because if there ever was a person I'd like to emulate, it's my dad," Claiborne Jr. explained. He described his father as "a kind, gentle, caring, sharing and giving individual. He gives of his time and wealth to everything."

Always considerate, Claiborne hates to inconvenience anyone, remembers Ann Carol. "Daddy did not want to make anybody wait. Daddy is almost obsessed with being on time or early to a meeting in order that other people not wait."

Punctuality was a constant challenge for the children. Claiborne made an effort to teach it almost every morning when he cooked breakfast for Lora and the children — "bacon and eggs or whatever," said Betty. "I remember Daddy calling us repeatedly to come down to breakfast so we wouldn't be late for school."

"One thing Daddy used to do is to tell us it was, say, quarter to eight if it was 7:30," said Ann Carol. "He would always say it was later to light a firecracker under us."

To Ann Carol, Claiborne was a kind and loving father, "the kind of man you could always talk to. He took me to all the baseball games the same way he took my brother. He didn't treat me like this prissy little female who had to stay home and put on make-up.

"One of his characteristics that I value so much is his ability to keep a confidence," said Ann Carol. "It taught me trust. He once told me that if I wanted to keep something secret, don't even tell one person. He taught me that if you are told something in confidence, you do not repeat it.

"Daddy was determined we were not going to be brats," she said. "He used to tell us when we acted up that we sounded like

Elvira Snitchinplant, and we knew we were being reprimanded."

Betty agreed. "Most frequently he would let us know how disappointed he was in our behavior, and there couldn't have been an incentive that meant more to us than his approval.

"I remember difficult times as a teenager," remembered Betty, "when my strong-willed nature clashed terribly with Mother, and how Daddy's calm logic and Martha Scott's loving comfort together helped to make those teenage years more bearable. Martha couldn't and Daddy wouldn't take a stand contrary to Mother's.

"Mother's word was generally law when it came to household matters. Daddy's primary influence on us was in showing his disappointment in us when one of us had an ethical lapse," said Betty.

"He taught us mainly by example how to be a good person. Mother did the disciplining, and the only time I remember Daddy losing his temper with me was when I would talk disrespectfully to him. That he would not tolerate. He disciplined us with a disappointed, 'Oh, sweetie,' except when I talked with him disrespectfully, when he would get so angry he would hit me, usually on my backside.

"I was particularly impressed by his example of generosity and tolerance. In an era where exclusive clubs were the norm, he practically single-handedly spearheaded the effort to break the barrier against Jews belonging to the Commonwealth Club."

Claiborne's fairness, consideration and gentility often came through his example. "He was constantly on the alert to be aware of other people's feelings and to be tolerant of the viewpoints of others," said Ann Carol, who also recalled Claiborne's affection.

"Daddy has never had any trouble in showing appreciation openly, and so many people can't do that. He is physically demonstrative, always patting us, putting his arm around us, and I just love that about him. His gentle, sensitive side is so extraordinary, so atypical of men."

IX

TRAVELS

Claiborne's first trip to New York City as a 13-year-old inspired a lifelong fascination with travel. For business and pleasure he saw the world and discovered tremendous rewards from diverse cultures and exotic landscapes.

Claiborne's first foray into business travels, aside from his many detailing trips, occurred shortly after World War II, when professional organizations began scheduling conventions that were as enjoyable as they were informative.

"The American Pharmaceutical Manufacturer's Association had their first convention after the war — it was '46, I believe — and they got a private train from Chicago to Lake Louise. The whole convention was on this train, and it was about a two-day and two-night trip in those days, so all of us met in Chicago, and what a rockin' trip that was," laughed Claiborne.

"Fortunately, we had a coach, a pullman coach, toward the back of the train, so we could go back there and get away from it, but that was a continuous party for two days. It was really rockin', I tell you. There must have been more alcohol consumed per capita on that train than on many a train in many a day.

"It was our first year that we were members of the association, so we were sort of greenhorns, and we didn't know many people, but we met a lot of people, and when you are confined on a train for two days and two nights, you really get to know people, and you know who are the ones who party the most and who don't," he chuckled.

"One thing I remember, and it struck me as being funny at the time, there was a young man on there named Wally Morrison. I remember him so well, one of the few people I remember real well from that trip. He was not a member; he was a supplier, and he was with the Illinois Water Treatment Company out of Rockville, Illinois, and he was the first thing on the program when the convention opened.

"After two days of partying on the train the program opened promptly at 9:00. Wally Morrison opened the program. Well, he looked up and he suddenly realized that the only people there to attend his lecture were the people he had met and had been closest to on the train. So he got up and he looked around and he says, 'Well, good morning section hands of car 481,'" laughed Claiborne, "which, of course, got a roar out of us. Sure enough, we were the only ones that got up to hear his speech."

During a later trip to Canada that included Lake Louise, Claiborne and Lora stayed at the Princess Hotel in Victoria, British Columbia on Vancouver Island. They had tea on the wide veranda that wraps around the beautiful old hotel. "Lunch there was a very beautiful experience," Claiborne said, who reflected on Canada.

"One of the things I recall from that trip, we decided we would go over to Banff, which is a sister hotel. I was not much of a golfer in those days, but I saw what a gorgeous course that was, so I decided to play golf, and I have never seen such a gorgeous setting in my life — the mountains were around you and the peaks and the rushing streams through the middle of the course.

"I said that it was the only time in my life that I could fully, truthfully say that I didn't play very well because I was so busy looking at the scenery that I couldn't watch the ball. I would say that the two most beautiful courses that I have ever had the privilege of seeing or even playing on are Pebble Beach and Banff.

"Canadians pride themselves on being different, but they are not as different, perhaps, as they think," he said. "Most U.S. companies have plants in Canada. We had a plant in Montreal that supplied Canada because the dues were pretty heavy for medicines coming in and out of Canada. We did very well there, always very profitable.

"Canada is, of course, two countries divided by two languages. Montreal is a very interesting city, good food, and more French in flavor. Vancouver is a beautiful city, not as pretty as Hong Kong, but nice. It's a good place to do business, and the Canadian Rockies are gorgeous."

In 1949, Claiborne and Lora were off to Europe on their first international trip. They had sailed from New York on the Queen Mary, and in England they visited Westminster Cathedral and watched the changing of the guard at Windsor Castle.

They appreciated the English countryside with its neat cottages and verdant landscape, typical of Shakespeare country. On later trips to London they stayed at the Savoy, where they would never forget the meticulous, personalized service the hotel provided its guests.

Leaving England for the continent, however, bizarre circumstances made for a frightful incident.

"We were scheduled to take a ferry at a point north of London, so we took the train up to this point and we were to go over to Holland on an overnight ferry," explained Claiborne. "When we got ready to retire, we noticed that the door was warped. We thought we had the door locked and we went to sleep, and in the middle of the night — I don't know what time it was — but all of a sudden I was awakened by somebody choking me to death.

"Of course, I opened my eyes, and there was this huge Englishman, he looked like he was about 6' 6", and he was literally choking me to death, and, of course, I was taken by surprise coming out of a sleep, so I didn't even have time to defend myself. Well, my wife got hold of the alarm bell and started ringing it. It made a loud noise, and not a soul showed up, not a soul. They were all asleep, and they didn't bother about it.

"She, fortunately, had presence of mind enough to get a shoe, the first thing she put her hands on, and she had the thing up above her head. She was just about to conk him over the back of the head, and he looked and saw her about to assault him with that shoe.

"Apparently, he was drunk. He had been drinking in the bar, and he had come back and decided that we were in his bunk. Anyway, when he saw that shoe and that woman about to hit him over the head, he realized he was in the wrong spot, and he got out of there in a hurry. Well, anyway, that was our first traumatic experience on our first trip to Europe."

Deciding not to press charges, the couple traveled to Switzerland for visits in Lucerne and Interlocken, where Claiborne and Lora took in the majestic alpine scenery. Claiborne was, above all, fascinated by the efficiency of Switzerland.

"The trains, as well as the watches, run right on the second," he said, having bought a watch for only $18.50. "I still have it. I don't use it much, you have to wind it every three days or so, but I still use it when another watch is being repaired. It's still running after 50 years or so."

They took the train over the Alps to Italy and stopped at Lake Como for a night, then moved on to Venice where they visited a glass works on a nearby island, and prowled the city.

They had mixed feelings about Venice: "In Venice the canals are filthy ... everything was moldy. All the buildings have that musty feeling. Maybe we just had the wrong hotel, but you got the feeling that no one ever went to bed. Of course, Florence is our love. Florence, to me, is the highlight of Italy. I would love to go back to Florence at any time.

"Two or three things struck me as being rather remarkable about Italy; it shows you the difference in culture. I remember this because we were so startled. They are very relaxed about bathroom facilities, and we were startled to see that many places in Italy along the wall they'd have open latrines, right out there in the open. They didn't try to disguise it.

"I remember, as we left Rome, we had a bus that was to take us across the Italian Riviera to Nice, to the French Riviera, and they suggested, since it was a fairly long bus ride, that we go to the bathroom just before we got on the bus. So I went to the desk clerk and asked him where the bathroom was and he pointed to one door — there couldn't be any question to where he pointed — and just as I got to the door, two ladies came out, and that kind of startled me, so I went to the desk clerk again to see if I had misunderstood him.

"He said, 'No, that's it, right there.' So I barged on in, and inside were several men and several ladies. Some of them were doing their faces. Of course they had stalls, but otherwise there was no effort to separate the sexes at all. That was kind of a revelation, shall I say, but I suppose you get used to that pretty quick. But it just shows you the difference in cultures. They don't think anything about it. Maybe they are healthier than we are in that respect.

"I don't know why I remember this," he chuckled, "but I used to have an occasional martini before dinner, and Florence was the only place in Europe where I got a good martini, I remember that. We were in Denmark a few years later and I ordered a very dry martini. Well, it came and I tasted it and it tasted horrible. Horrible! I sent it back and got another one, and the same thing came back. It turns out the waiter interpreted that I wanted Martini & Rossi straight vermouth. Well, if there is anything that I don't like it's straight vermouth. Finally, I got my martini by ordering that they bring me a bottle of gin and let me fix my own," he laughed, "which they finally did."

From Venice the tour moved on to Rome, and then boarded a bus for Genoa, from where it traveled over the Italian Alps to Nice. The bus caught up with a bicycle race and had to follow the pumping cyclists. It delayed the bus by a couple of hours. In Nice, the Robinses expected to see many of the bikini bathing suits then becoming vogue, but the weather did not cooperate.

"We stayed at the Negresco, a fine old hotel, still there," said Claiborne. "We had a nice stay in Nice, but one thing struck me as being funny. At that time, bikinis were very popular in France, and they hadn't quite taken hold then in the states, but women were sort of a sensation in bikinis and less, and so we naturally thought we'd run into that in Nice, being the great resort that it is.

"Well, we hit a cold snap. The two days we were in Nice, I think the highest the temperature got was about 58 and the lowest about 48, and this was just about the first of June. Much to my disappointment, not one bikini was to be seen, not a soul was on the beach. Everybody had on sweaters. So my first trip to Nice was completely without bikinis," he said disappointedly.

From Nice they took the express train overnight to Paris to take in the cultural offerings of one of Europe's greatest cities. Surprisingly, at the Rodin museum, they found a friend from Richmond, and another Richmonder was at the performance of the Folies Bergére.

"Paris, of course, is my favorite city of all cities," said Claiborne. "It is a beautiful city, and for a big city it is remarkably clean. The food, of course, is excellent. You have a wide choice of foods, every kind of restaurant in the world is in Paris, and most of it is surprisingly good. I suppose it's because the competition is so keen. If you aren't good, you don't survive. Even the so-called inexpensive restaurants are good."

The intricacies of enjoying the French restaurants were soon mastered. "I quickly learned that if you try to make a reservation at a French restaurant they can be sold out, but if you have a French friend who will call, you can get in.

"We found out something else about French restaurants," he said. "If you had a great meal at one and told them so, they usually had room for you if you wanted to come back two nights later. And, of course the concierges can be very helpful if they are generously tipped," he added.

"On this '49 trip, the first trip that we took, we felt very guilty because, even though it was about three years after the war, they had not anywhere near fully recovered from the war. In

England, we saw a lot of the evidences of the destruction from the bombing. They hadn't been able to build things back.

"When we were served meals in the better hotels or the better restaurants, they always had us partitioned off with a screen so the other people in the restaurant could not see what we were having for dinner, because they were serving the tourists the best that they had available, but they still had not recovered enough to serve the average patron what we would have — lamb chops, for example, which no one else in England or France had at the time."

Despite the ravages of war, it was the many attractions of Paris that inspired Claiborne most of all. He and Lora followed the Seine's lazy meanderings, strolling along the flowered walkways and resting in a particularly pretty nook alongside the river. Lora and Claiborne smiled at the couples stretched out in the grass and walking hand in hand by the Seine's romantic banks, and they saw a great deal of art.

"There are more museums in Paris than in any other city in the world," said Claiborne. "It is truly the artist center of the world. You could spend months there, take one museum a day, and not get around to all of them. You could spend two weeks in the Louvre alone, if you were that interested.

"I've been to Paris six or seven times. If I'm in Europe at all I try to make a point to get in Paris at least two or three days, and hopefully, more if I can. I've never been disappointed. That's the interesting thing about Paris, I've always heard that the Parisians are very rude, and yet I've never run into that. I think it's because of how you handle it. If you treat people with respect, it is usually rewarded.

"My favorite nightclub there, of course, is the Crazy Horse, which I have been back to several times. It has been running for, gosh, I reckon ... heavens ... 40 years, and they are still going strong.

"The Crazy Horse is the most innovative and delightful strip joint that you would ever want to go to. The French have a particular knack for presentation, so we'd say. They do it in a very elegant ... I don't think elegant is the word because the material is not elegant ... but they do it with such finesse that nobody really could be offended.

"Last time I was there I took my children. I think they were in their late teens. Of course, it's just packed every night. They have two performances a night. I have never been in a place where they put as many people in the same room. You are so crowded that they have these little tables; you can only get one drink apiece on the table, and there isn't any room for anything else, and everybody is in everybody else's lap, and nobody minds.

"I remember one time," he chuckled, "this is something that just popped into my mind. I had long forgotten about it. We were over there later on another trip, and our host for the evening was a pharmaceutical company executive who was hoping to do some business with us, and we were hoping to do some business with him.

"He took us out to dinner, and he said, afterwards, 'Would you like to go to a little different nightclub?' and we said, sure, you know, innocent that we were. So we went to a nightclub. Well, we get there and it turns out that it's a lesbian nightclub. All these men were dressed up like women, and women were dressed up like men, and you didn't know who was who.

"Anyway, we hadn't been there very long before one of them came up to my wife and said, 'Wouldn't you like to dance?' She said, 'No, I don't dance.' She did dance, but she said, 'No, thank you,'" laughed Claiborne. "Well, I remember that was quite an experience, I'd never been to a place like that, but it was obvious what it was after we got there, but we still weren't quite sure who was who.

"Maybe they were all women, I don't know. Maybe the women just dressed as women and were lesbians, or they were dressed as men and pretended that they were. But anyway, it was very confusing, and that was the only time that we got to that type of place.

"Paris is a very relaxed city, but being married, I didn't have the opportunity to take advantage of any of the opportunities, but I didn't have any particular desire to, incidentally. But there are a number of places there that are generally known to be available for trysts.

"They are built for that purpose, and the French — I think French women must be very blasé about their husbands — they all know that they've got a mistress, and apparently it's accepted, and I would guess that nine-tenths of the men over there have a mistress somewhere — they seemed to be relaxed about it. I know it was true years ago. I can't say what it is today."

French connections were never any trouble for Claiborne, as A. H. Robins had two companies there. Paris was the home office for Caron Parfums and a pharmaceutical firm, Martinet, which was located just outside the city.

As much as he liked Paris, there was one thing that irritated him. "I don't think I've ever been to France that one group or another wasn't on strike. It's the bus drivers, airline employees, railroad workers or electricians, or somebody. It's frustrating."

Claiborne and Lora returned to the U.S. on the Queen Elizabeth, traveling in splendor and basking in memories of European experiences that were to be shared with the children when, years later, Claiborne took the family to England when the children were in their teens. A Richmond friend had just returned from there and had recommended the guide he had employed. Claiborne got the same guide, a young woman in her 20s.

"She knew London and England backwards and forwards," he said. "We had a wonderful experience; she knew where to go, how to get in places without waiting. She drove us up to Stonehenge and the Shakespeare country."

Claiborne was fascinated with Stonehenge. "The mystery is still how they got them there," he said of the huge rock monoliths. "They obviously came from a long way off, yet no one knows how they got there. It was quite a sight."

Claiborne was interested in the many English pubs. "They have surprisingly good food in the pubs. They are warm, usually one of the only places in England where you can get warm."

In the 1970s, Claiborne Jr. and his wife joined Lora and Claiborne on a trip to Europe, traveling in the Concorde. They stayed three days in Paris, then went to Monaco, to the Hotel de Paris, right across the street from the Casino de Monte Carlo, where they spent a few dollars on the slot machines.

"From Nice to Monte Carlo there are three roads, with a second level higher and a third level very high. It gives you a scenic view that is unusual," said Claiborne. "Coming back from Monte Carlo, we had lunch in the famous Eden Roc restaurant, right down on the Mediterranean, Cap Antibes. I had a seat overlooking the swimming pool, and the topless ladies were all around," he said with a twinkle.

Venturing into southern Europe, Lora and Claiborne went to Greece and hired a professor of Greek history as their guide. They stayed at the Athens Hilton, a new hotel at the time, which overlooked the Acropolis.

The professor asked them if they'd mind being late getting back to the hotel one night so that he could show them a rare sight. They agreed, and they set out from Athens and drove 40 minutes, and then walked up to some ancient ruins at Cape Sounion. "In about 20 minutes," the professor said, "you're going to see something spectacular."

As darkness fell, the professor said, "Look to the left and then look to the right." On one side the sun was sinking into the water and on the other the moon was rising. "It was quite an experience," Claiborne said.

The Greek people were friendly, but the airport worried the Robinses. "It was a madhouse, with a couple of thousand people screaming at each other," said Claiborne. "You couldn't find anyone who would tell you where a gate was, and they did not tell you at the ticket counter. I'll never forget that visit to the Athens airport." The Robinses managed to find their plane and flew to Beirut, Lebanon.

"We had a business meeting in Lebanon," said Claiborne, "a sales meeting for sales reps from all over the Middle East. Beirut was, at that time, the meeting place for Arabs to gamble and have a good time. It was prosperous, a big commercial city. Everybody seemed to get along, and they did a lot of business. The reps were from Iran, Iraq, Jordan, and all the Arab countries. They got along fine, with great good fellowship. It was a great sales meeting," he said.

Claiborne's party went into a gambling casino, "the most marvelous I have ever seen," he said. "The greatest nightclub floor show I have ever seen was there. It must have cost them a couple of million dollars to put it on."

Performers of mixed nationalities swung into elaborate choral productions while gamblers spent fortunes at the gaming tables. "Some of the Arab sheiks thought nothing of risking a million dollars on one throw of the dice," he said.

Claiborne knew a Richmonder in Beirut, a doctor who practiced in both Beirut and Richmond. An obstetrician and gynecologist, Dr. Bickers, had quite a reputation in Lebanon and treated the Arab royalty from that part of the world. He had the confidence of the wealthy Arabs, and since some of the native physicians were not trusted, he had an elite clientele.

He hosted dinner for Claiborne and his party one night during the sales meeting. Claiborne brought the latest news from Richmond and the United States, and Dr. Bickers helped the Americans understand the Arab culture.

There were trips around the U.S., too, and Claiborne liked Las Vegas, with its neon glitter, great shows, and the best in nightclub entertainers. The gambling was never a temptation, however. "It's a great place for an inexpensive education, if you don't gamble. I confined my gambling to the slot machine and I always had a policy of a maximum of $100," said Claiborne, "and

Lora and Claiborne in Las Vegas.

if I lost that, I quit! Even when you hit the jackpot on the second try, which I've done, you'll put it right back in. In the stock market, at least you've got a 50/50 chance."

Claiborne and Lora were invited to the Army-Navy game in Philadelphia one year and decided to go, accompanied by Mallory and Mary Freeman. They caught the train in Richmond at 5 a.m. and were met in Philadelphia by Doug Sterns, an advertising representative with whom they did business.

At the stadium, they saw Navy's great quarterback, Roger Stauback, who later starred for the Dallas Cowboys in the National Football League. Army's great combination of Doc Blanchard and Glen Davis had rolled over all their opposition that year, but Stauback's play thrilled Claiborne.

"He almost single-handedly beat Army," said Claiborne, who said it was a great day to indulge his interest in sports, enhanced by the pageantry of the cadets from the nation's two great military academies. The train to Richmond got them back that night at 10 p.m., tired but happy.

Claiborne loved flying and was very comfortable on airplanes. "One of the amazing things in life is that you are safer flying on a scheduled airliner than you are on the ground. When you think of the millions of flights going on all over the world and how few accidents there are, it is remarkable. You're probably three times safer in the air than in an automobile," he said.

One flight, from Manila to Seattle, he remembered particularly well: "Northwest Airlines initiated a service between Manila and Seattle; a long, long flight. There were two stops, one in Okinawa and one in Tokyo, then non-stop from Tokyo to Seattle. I boarded the plane around 3:30 p.m. in Manila, and I was the only one on the plane. Just before take-off another man got aboard, so there were two passengers for the flight.

"We got to Okinawa and spent 30 minutes there, and still no one got on. I thought, well surely more passengers will board at Tokyo. This service is new and people haven't got used to it yet. But no one got on at Tokyo. So there we were with two stewardesses and two passengers on this plane big enough to cross the Pacific. I decided to introduce myself to the other passenger. Ironically, he was a tobacco buyer from Richmond.

"When we got to Seattle, we circled and circled in a thick fog. After a while we were sent to Portland to refuel. Finally, they flew back to Seattle, but the fog had closed in again. At 2:30 p.m. the plane put down at Boeing's airfield south of Seattle, and we were bussed to Seattle to the customs office. We had spent almost 24 hours on that plane, and I was dead tired. It was incredible that only two people were on a flight of that duration, both from the same place."

After having visited Asia, Claiborne wanted Lora to share his experiences. On a memorable trip, they went to Bangkok and Hong Kong, and then to Japan. They landed at Osaka and had reservations for a hotel in Kyoto, 25 miles north. Claiborne described Kyoto as having wide streets, lovely avenues, and many shrines. It is meticulously maintained, he said, and is one of the art centers of Japan.

They marveled at the oriental ability to create beauty and serenity, and shopped for gifts to take back home. They taxied from their hotel to a restaurant and had a delightful meal. Only one Japanese person spoke English the entire time. They took the bullet train from Kyoto back to Tokyo, a 300-mile trip.

"The Japanese pride themselves on their bullet trains, and

Lora learns to dance the hula on a trip to Hawaii circa 1960.

they have a right to do so, because those things run 175 miles an hour or so, and they run on time," said Claiborne.

Their destination was Hakone, a little town at the foot of Mt. Fuji, where they were to spend the night. The A. H. Robins agent in Tokyo was their host in Japan, and he offered to drive over to Hakone to meet them and take them to the hotel.

Claiborne and Lora boarded the bullet train, mingling with the crowd of Japanese in western and native dress, and settled down for the trip in the beautifully decorated and immaculate car. The train left the station, gathering speed as the Japanese scenery flashed by. Lora and Claiborne peered through the windows at the neat countryside.

They had gone 50 or 60 miles when the train slowed to a stop. They waited 20 minutes, moved a few miles, and stopped. This pattern repeated itself several times, and finally Claiborne asked another traveler what had happened. An accident, he was told. A bullet train ahead of theirs had smashed into a dump truck, derailed and torn up 100 yards of track and a bridge.

Repairs would take hours, they were told, so the Robinses joined most of the other passengers in the diner for lunch and again, later, for dinner. What had started as a two- to three-hour trip now had stretched out to ten hours, and the resources of the dining car were being exhausted.

"I'll never forget this," said Claiborne. "We had a bottle of liquor that somebody had given us, and the train was running out of food and drink, so we offered some Scotch to the Japanese sitting around us, and soon they brought us sandwiches. They had brought food with them rather than buy it on the train, and they wanted to share it. I was touched by that. It gave us an insight into the Japanese people. They were very ashamed of their bullet train and kept apologizing for the accident, and kept bringing us wine and sandwiches."

The train started moving again, and they watched as they passed over the wreck site, patched up enough to allow the train to move slowly through. "I was amazed that the Japanese could complete those repairs in ten hours or so," Claiborne said.

The train resumed its speed and roared down the track into Hakone. They had been scheduled to arrive at 3:30 in the afternoon, and it was nearly midnight when they arrived. Claiborne and Lora were impressed that their Japanese driver was still there, waiting to take them to their hotel.

The Japanese businessmen, as well as the ordinary citizen, made an impression on Claiborne. "They are exceedingly industrious, very smart as managers. They don't pay the highest wages, but they have the highest benefits in the world. Unions are virtually unknown, and that's one of their secrets. They don't have to contend with unions. The employees are very loyal, very dedicated to their companies.

"They also take a longer term approach. They usually don't worry about whether or not they are going to make money in the first year or two. Liability is not as much of a problem there. Lee Iacocca was quoted as saying that they have as many lawyers in

Japan as we have sumo wrestlers. Japan has a tremendous competitive advantage over us there."

Claiborne and Lora were entertained by the manager of a Robins subsidiary in Tokyo and went to a Kobe beef house. "It's the greatest beef in the world," said Claiborne. "They massage it, give it a special diet, and the beef is enormously expensive. You'd go down a narrow street, plain on the outside, but inside it would be very nice. The meal then was about $100 apiece, but it was the most delicious steak you ever put in your mouth. The Japanese had a lot of restaurants where you cooked your own. They put a pot of boiling water in front of you, and if you got a beef dinner, you dipped your slice in the water to suit your taste for rare, medium or well done. It was very good food and delicious meat."

Much closer to home, Mexico had become a favorite destination for Claiborne. It was close enough to Richmond to make a quick trip, but foreign enough to offer a diverse cultural shift.

"We had been to Acapulco the first time and stayed in a hotel," said Claiborne. "The second time we heard that John Wayne's place was for rent. He had this great place way up on a cliff overlooking the Pacific, a fabulous site. The food was excellent. They had four servants: a maid, cook, butler and gardener.

"Although the cook did not speak much English, she managed to give excellent meals and made it very pleasant. We were able to rent that gorgeous place with all those servants, and the only thing we paid was $600 a day for our party of nine. It was the treat of a lifetime.

"One time while we were there, they (the travel agency) called and asked if they could have a party there with a band, and so on, so we said, sure, and we joined the party. The sunsets were the most gorgeous. We'd gather every night and watch the sun go down into the water. We had a great time there.

"That trip was so interesting that we went back and stayed another time with the Browns, Freemans and Dick Velz. The sightseeing boat cruised by the house, and 1,500' up we could

Lora, Claiborne, Betty, Claiborne Jr. and Ann Carol in Acapulco in the early 1970s.

hear the loudspeaker describing John Wayne's house. Velz would get up and wave, pretending he was John Wayne. Mexicans had a reverence for John Wayne.

"We also invited the Thomases — Dr. Warren Thomas and his wife. We chartered an Eastern Airlines Jet Star and flew to Acapulco, the nine of us. We were there for two weeks, and the charter was for the jet to come back and pick us up at 12 noon on the day of departure. But word got back to us from Eastern that one of the Eastern bigwigs had commandeered the Jet Star. They wanted to take us back at 9 p.m., instead of noon. That would put us back in Richmond after midnight, maybe at 2 a.m.

"We told them that we thought they should honor the contract. Eastern agreed, and when we showed up at the Acapulco airport, there was a 727 waiting to take us home," Claiborne said. They flew non-stop from Acapulco to Richmond in three hours, a record time with the help of a strong tail wind.

Later, Claiborne became close friends with Floyd Hall, president of Eastern Airlines, whom he had met on the first *Time* magazine trip he took. "You meet just one person and it changes the course of your life in some ways," said Claiborne. "It happens time and time again."

A pleasant and unexpected surprise occurred when Claiborne wanted to go to Dorado Beach, Puerto Rico, a Caribbean beach-front paradise with gambling and entertainment about 20 miles west of San Juan. The facility, at that time, was controlled by the Rockefellers, who also controlled Eastern Airlines. When Claiborne wrote for reservations, he was told that nothing was available, so he wrote Floyd Hall and asked him if there was anything Floyd could do to help him get on a waiting list.

The next morning he was told that he had a reservation. They flew down on Eastern. At the desk in the resort they were told that they were expected. "We have a car available for you and you are in cottage no. 1," the desk clerk told him. Although the Robinses did not know it, cottage no. 1 was the Rockefeller cottage, owned by the Rockefellers themselves.

When Claiborne checked out, he was told that he was charged only for the meals, not for the cottage or the car. Surprised, Claiborne wrote his friend Floyd Hall to express his gratitude.

"As a result, I always flew Eastern Airlines, even when the schedules were not the most convenient. In fact, I rode Eastern Airlines up until the time they went bankrupt." The Robinses made several other visits to Dorado Beach over the years, and it remained one of Claiborne's favorite places.

Claiborne always appreciated good service, and usually responded with his loyalty in return. Pan American Airlines earned his appreciation on a flight to Europe.

"We were on Pan American — in fact, I always flew Pan Am whenever I went abroad, except when we went on the Concorde. We were on the way back from Germany and Switzerland and had scheduled two or three days in London. Lora fell ill and got so bad that we knew she couldn't fly.

"We notified the airline that we could not honor our reservations. Pan Am, on their own, made an appointment with the best gynecologist in England and a reservation for me near the hospital and near the airport, and furnished me a car." In a few days Lora was able to travel, and they flew home to Richmond.

Claiborne wrote the airline's president, detailed the services he had received, and expressed his appreciation, enduring loyalty, and determination to fly Pan American. Claiborne later learned that his letter was circulated to Pan Am's top people all over the world as an example of what service can do.

"The policy that I've always had, is that if someone treats me right, I am dedicated to doing business with him," explained Claiborne. "We've done business over the years with people who have been good to us, for example, suppliers. When things were very scarce, they saw to it that we got bottles or other supplies, and we made sure that we did business with them. It paid off for us. When we took Chapter 11, our suppliers stayed with us, and every one of them got paid," he said.

Claiborne was frequently off to some part of the world, either on business or simply because there was somewhere he had not been. In Europe he visited Switzerland, Germany, Italy, France, England, Luxembourg, Belgium, Holland, and Denmark. He did not venture into Eastern Europe, however.

"I've never had any desire to go behind the Iron Curtain, and I still don't. Our one visit to the border of Russia was enough to deter us. We had to declare every dollar. There are too many other beautiful places to go to first," said Claiborne.

Claiborne visited all of the Central American countries on one occasion alone when he was in Mexico City and had to go to Panama to take care of company business. He caught a local flight from Mexico City, not realizing that the plane would stop in almost every city in Central America. They put down in Nicaragua, Honduras, Guatemala, and several others, flying 20 or 30 minutes, and then spending a half hour on the ground.

In Venezuela he met the top government officials. "I guess they were hoping we would put a bigger plant there; we had a small one there. Mr. Tovar was head of the Venezuelan operation and he had connections with everybody in Venezuela, which is the way you operate in those countries. The government does so much of the buying, and if you don't have someone who knows the right people at the top, you're in trouble," Claiborne said.

He had business in Rio, and he and Lora invited Bill Brown and his wife to go along. Claiborne and Bill Brown were good friends, and Brown's company, W. M. Brown and Sons, did most of the printing for A. H. Robins. They traveled to the top of Sugar Loaf mountain for the spectacular view of one of the world's most beautiful harbors, and their hosts entertained them in royal style.

However, the great impression Rio left with Claiborne was the enormous gap between the rich and the poor. Rio's "pretty wild" during Carnival, said Claiborne, but it was pretty staid when the Robinses were there, "except for the bathing suits, the briefest in the world," Claiborne recalled. They left with the feeling that Rio was not a particularly friendly place.

The Browns also went along to Mardi Gras one year. They took the R. F. & P. Railroad to Washington D.C., and then the New Orleans train, and stayed at the St. Charles Hotel in the French Quarter. "We were fortunate to stay in that hotel," said Claiborne. "The hotel gave its guests priority to an area that overlooked the parade route. All the big parades came down the street, right by the hotel, and we saw them all from the second floor of the hotel. We had a great time in New Orleans."

Claiborne's three favorite cities in the world are Paris, Hong Kong and San Francisco. "Those three have great natural beauty and great food," he said.

Claiborne loved the trolley cars in San Francisco and the way people crowd into the cars and hang onto the sides. "It's a wonder some people don't fall off and kill themselves, but they never seem to," he said. "It's a relatively small city, and you can see most of its sights in a couple of days time." He took his family to Trader Vic's and other great restaurants there.

Hong Kong's beauty, laid out across the mountainside, lifted his spirits. "The skyscrapers are built right up on top of the mountains and overlook Hong Kong Harbor, one of the most beautiful in the world," Claiborne described. The water, teeming with junks, sailing yachts, freighters and passenger ships, was fascinating to him. "They have a half dozen of the finest hotels in the world," he said, adding that A. H. Robins had a small business there at the time.

While not his favorite spot to live, New York remained a special place to visit, and it was relatively close to Richmond. As a young man, Claiborne traveled there by train, sometimes even without a ticket.

"During World War II, to get a through train to New York was just almost impossible. I was determined to go to New York, anyway, to see a few shows. I suppose I shouldn't be proud of this," he chuckled, "but to show you my determination, I got up to New York, and I didn't have a ticket back. There wasn't a ticket available anywhere.

"In those days at Grand Central Station the crowds were so enormous. Everyone was traveling by train to save gas. I got a scheme to get back when not a ticket was to be had. I had noticed that when they opened the gates there was a surge of people. The ticket takers just gave up on trying to check anybody's ticket. I noticed that they just surged, so I decided to go down to the station and get in that surge, and when I went through, they didn't check any tickets.

"So I got on the train and I thought, well, where could I go where I wouldn't be in the way, so to speak. I thought about the lounge car. Of course, before you got to Philadelphia the conductor would come through to take up the tickets. When they came to me, I said, 'I am sorry, I just wasn't able to get a ticket before I left, but, of course, I expect to pay whatever the going rate is.'

"I pulled out my cash and he said, 'You know you shouldn't be on here without a ticket.' I said, 'I'm sorry about that.' He reluctantly accepted my cash, although he was still fussing about it, and so I did that at least twice and got away with it. One time, the conductor even threatened to put me off in Washington, which I took with a grain of salt, because I didn't think he would, and sure enough, they forgot about it. I paid for my ticket, of course."

Later, during family and business trips when the company had become more affluent, Claiborne usually got reservations at the Waldorf-Astoria. The December convention of the Pharmaceutical Manufacturers Association was often held at the Waldorf. He liked the hotel, but several times he had not been able to get into his room on arrival mid-afternoon because the room was not ready. On one occasion he could not get into his room until 8:00 at night. "I got tired of that," he said, "and never stayed there again."

The Barkley Hotel was right across the street from the Waldorf, and Claiborne found the personnel and accommodations to be excellent. "We stayed there for ten or 15 years in a row before we started going to the Plaza, and never once did I have any trouble with a reservation.

"Small things make an impression," said Claiborne. "Several

Claiborne and Lora in New York City in the 1950s.

times I walked into the Barkley and signed my name, and the man behind the desk recognized the name and said, 'Mister Allbee with C!,' and I said he was right and that I took one every day. He replied that he did too. That alone was enough to make you want to come back."

Claiborne and Lora were at the Barkley for a few days one December when a 15-inch snowstorm paralyzed the city. No traffic could move in the city. Sak's Fifth Avenue was just a couple of blocks away, and Claiborne got restless one morning. He walked over to the great store and found it open for business.

"I remember walking in, and I was about the only customer in there. They had a few clerks who had gotten in somehow, and I never had as much attention in my life."

Claiborne recalled one trip he made to Denver on business and told of a trip he would never forget: "The most interesting taxi ride I ever had in my life; we were out in Denver. I was with Dave Robbins and I was to get an award out there from Beta Gamma Sigma, and so we went out and had a nice dinner, and we came out and we hailed a taxi, and we got into the taxi and gave the hotel, and the taxi driver looks around and says, 'Do you like music?'"

"We said, sure we love music! So we thought he was going to turn on the radio, but he reaches under the seat and pulls out a trumpet, and he proceeds to get that thing up in front of him — he doesn't have any hands on the wheel. He drove us the whole way downtown, which I guess was 25 minutes, playing that trumpet the whole way, and we were so petrified we didn't know whether to enjoy the music or not!"

Whether for business or pleasure, foreign or domestic, Claiborne benefited from the expanding view of the world he achieved through travel. From the time he had won his trip to New York City by selling magazines as a boy, Claiborne knew he wanted to see as much of the world as he could. He fulfilled that dream, and nothing in his life, other than his joy in seeing his money benefit others, gave Claiborne more pleasure than travel.

X

TIME MAGAZINE

In 1965 and 1969 Claiborne saw a tumultuous part of the world like few others when he was honored by *Time* magazine as one of the nation's top businessmen. The publication took four news tours between 1963 and 1969 and Claiborne, along with other American business leaders, was invited to go along on two of those trips, touring the Far East.

The tours, according to *Time* publisher James Shepley, were "an attempt to provide a group of leading American businessmen and a number of executives of our own company with a direct experience in the Far East — journalistic inquiry, rather than commercial or economic intelligence. The members of the party went as responsible, concerned American citizens rather than as representatives of their business enterprises."

Most of the tour members were presidents or board chairmen of major U.S. firms. In 1969 there were 25 businessmen representing companies that altogether employed 2.4 million people and had sales totaling more than $55 billion.

"I never in my wildest dreams thought that *Time* would pick me to be one of 25 CEOs in the country to go on those trips," said an astounded Claiborne. "The only way I can account for it is that I had made a point to recognize *Time* in our Bowl of Hygeia awards. We had cover pictures made of the award recipients, and we invited a *Time* representative each year to the dinner. We were an advertiser, but not a big advertiser. I suppose that's how I got on the trip; because they were looking for a few small businessmen, and I was one of them."

Claiborne's first tour in 1965 was a three-week trip covering 25,000 miles. The magazine made no demands of the tour members, and the briefings were thorough and lengthy. The businessmen were encouraged to ask any question that came to mind. The answers would give an insight into the thinking of the leaders of each country they visited. Top officials of the Defense and State departments, and the CIA, briefed the business leaders in Washington, D.C.

"They made the arrangements but we paid our own way," Claiborne said. "We had an Air France plane, the same one that had been assigned to General DeGaulle, with his top pilots and stewardesses. Our skipper had 24,000 hours flying time."

The tour left New York and arrived in Paris just before midnight. There was a briefing for the businessmen over a late supper. They left Paris midday for Pakistan and arrived at Karachi around 9 p.m. Pakistan's President, Field Marshal Mohammed Ayub Kahn, subjected the tour to a bitter outburst over U.S. aid to India, and showed little warmth to his visiting dignitaries, who then traveled on to India.

Claiborne was stunned by the incredible poverty of India. Riding through New Delhi, he saw beggars lining the streets that led to magnificent government buildings, and it gave him a poor impression of the country. "The Indians themselves seemed not to care about the starving people," said Claiborne. "If they had help for the poor, it was so buried by the sheer amount of the poverty that it was not noticeable."

The *Time* travelers were entertained by top government officials, but Claiborne was not impressed. "Although they obviously did the best they could, the food was mediocre. I went down for breakfast one morning and they had pancakes on the menu, so I ordered pancakes. I wish you could have seen them. Have you had one of the hard rolls that you have a hard time sinking your teeth into? Well, that's the way these pancakes were. They were so tough that you ate them like a hard roll. I finally gave up and got a piece of toast." At a reception that evening at one of the top clubs in the city, the food was equally poor. "You wouldn't want to go back for it," he said.

Another apparent characteristic of the Indian people depressed Claiborne as much as the dirt and poverty. "I did not see a smile in all of India. I don't know if it's a national trait, or whether they considered it a trait of weakness, or what. Someone said that they didn't have much to smile about. We left there feeling that we weren't very welcome, although the outward facade of the Indian personality just seemed to be bleak."

Claiborne and the other businessmen heard Indian government officials discuss the possibility of foreign investment, but India's 65 percent tax on profits squelched any interest for most of the visitors. India also required that an Indian national own at least 51 percent of the business, no matter who put up the capital. All equipment had to have an import license, and equipment purchases had to go through the Indian bureaucracy. "None of us left there feeling like we'd like to invest in India," remarked Claiborne.

Next they flew into Thailand, landing at Bangkok. Rulers there stressed the need for the U.S. to stand firm in its struggle with Vietnam, warning that Thailand could not stand on its own. The exotic food included Ho Mok Poo, served to the accompaniment of dancing girls and tinkling bells. Claiborne enjoyed the oriental city with its 300 temples.

At Singapore's famous Raffles Hotel, the travelers heard Prime Minister Lee Quan Yew deliver a sharp criticism of U.S. policy. If the U.S. failed to hold Vietnam, he warned, there would be no choice for many small Far East nations but to go communist.

They moved on to the capital of Malaysia, Kuala Lumpur, for the 62nd birthday party of the Prime Minister Tunku Abdul Rahman, then back to Singapore for a briefing by British officials. Claiborne was impressed with Singapore's efficiency and excellent accommodations. During the trip, Claiborne found a friend in Floyd Hall, president of Eastern Airlines, and instead of touring more of Malaysia, they spent their time touring Singapore.

"They had beautiful hotels, several of the finest in the world there," he said, adding that crime was unknown in Singapore. "We were entertained by the Prime Minister of Singapore. Wong Kong Lee, or whatever his name is, has done an amazing job in Singapore. He entertained us at the famed Raffles Hotel. He is a very interesting guy, and he runs that place with an iron fist, and everybody does what he says, and they love him. I don't know how he manages that, but he does. He even holds down the population. One child, I think is allowed. You can have two, but it costs you plenty if you do."

Hong Kong was the next stop, and Claiborne was impressed. "An amazing country. Chinese work like beavers." The British authorities entertained the travelers, and, according to Claiborne, their success in Hong Kong comes from an intolerance of crime and drugs, and a laissez-faire attitude toward business, which has free reign. "We took the tram that goes up the side of the mountain with that magnificent view. Hong Kong is one of the miracles of the world," he said.

They flew on to Taiwan, where they were entertained by President and Mrs. Chaing Kai Shek at their official residence, Scholars Grove. At 5 p.m. the Gimo appeared wearing his famous khaki wool tunic and trousers. Madam Chaing wore a brocaded, plum-colored formal Chipao, a modified Manchu-style gown with a high collar. She immediately charmed Claiborne with her reply at his introduction: "It is so nice to hear a Southern accent again." She had attended a school in Georgia before entering Wellesley College. "It was a memorable moment," he said.

They took a side trip to Quemoy, at that time said to be the most heavily armed island in the world. The solid rock fortification was formidable, and designed to hold off the Red Chinese. They flew to Quemoy on old World War II Nationalist Air Force planes, the trusty DC 3s. "It looked like we were flying only about six feet over the water, and we asked about it," said Claiborne. "We were told that they flew low so the Red Chinese radar wouldn't pick them up."

From the top of the fortification they gazed through binoculars at Red Chinese troops across the channel on the mainland. Conversation turned to chances of the Reds shelling Quemoy, which they did occasionally. An official told them not to worry about it: "The Communists shell us on Mondays, Wednesdays and Fridays, just to remind us they are there. This is a Tuesday. No problem."

They flew back to Taiwan, and the next day were on their way to Japan. In Tokyo, they felt more at ease and soon turned attention to trade between Japan and the U.S. On the last leg, it was Claiborne's turn to ride in the cockpit of the 747, and he was awed by the approach and landing in San Francisco.

"This was about 3:00 in the morning," said Claiborne. "I had no idea of the complexity of the cockpit instruments. Even these experienced pilots used a checklist. They must have had 30 things on that list. You realize what a meticulous thing flying one of those big planes is. First you saw a little blip on the radar, and as you got closer, it began to fill in. Then you could see the lights of San Francisco. It was very thrilling."

The plane went on to New York, but Claiborne met Lora in San Francisco for a few days there, and then they flew back to Hawaii for a week at the Mona Kea Beach Resort on the Kona

Lora and Claiborne in Hawaii.

Coast of the Big Island. Claiborne and Lora stretched out on the sand, and he told her about his adventures.

When the invitation came from *Time* for the second news tour of the Far East, Claiborne wasted no time accepting. *Time* hosted the CEOs at the Fairmont Hotel in San Francisco on February 20, 1969, and the businessmen boarded their chartered Pan American Boeing 707 jet the next day for the flight to Honolulu. The entire trip covered 22,582 miles, 13 cities, and eight countries.

The *Time* group lost a day on the long flight to Manila, where they were housed in the Sheraton Hotel. There they were entertained by President Ferdinand Marcos and his wife Imelda, and Marcos gave the visitors a summary of the situation in the Philippines. The group was to go on the next day to Vietnam, but General Abrams, had suggested they delay the visit for a day.

"We got word that the bombing was right severe around Saigon and they would postpone our trip one day," said Claiborne. "Now, that didn't exactly make us feel easier, but when we got there the next night at the hotel we could hear the bombing, we were so close to it.

"When President Marcos and Mrs. Marcos, Imelda, heard that we were gonna be there another day, they invited the entire group of 30 businessmen, and these were the heads of AT&T, General Motors, G.E., Seagrams, and Phillip Morris — you never saw such an array of people.

"They invited us to go on their yacht so we went with them and it was a delightful day, and, of course, he had an enormous yacht, and they spent the whole day with us. But what startled us when we got there on the boat, all of a sudden we were met by these beautiful girls ... there were about 30 beautiful ... and I mean they were really stunners.

"We thought to ourselves, 'Where in the world, in one day's notice, did he come up with 30 such beautiful girls?' Well, it turns out that Mrs. Marcos had gotten the word the night before, and around midnight or thereabouts she called all of these girls who were beauty queens, who had won beauty contests around the Philippines and around the world, and she called their homes and said, 'We want you at 9:00 in the morning to be at the docks to go on this trip.' But some of them said, 'But I have engagements.' Mrs. Marcos said, 'Would you just as a favor to me be there?' They all showed up. There were no excuses accepted. That's what one of the girls told us, anyway."

The extra day was filled with a cruise on the 280 ft. presidential yacht. A Filipino band played under an awning on the fantail and there were tables with red tablecloths and a huge buffet. It was a very pleasant trip to Corregidor, where everything had been left as it was when General Douglas MacArthur left during World War II. Every gun placement and cannon was in place.

"You felt as if you had arrived just a couple of days after everybody had left," Claiborne said. In late afternoon they returned to the Sheraton and dressed for dinner, where there was music, food and Filipino dances.

Claiborne found another touching scene in the Philippines. They visited the American cemetery outside Manila, and there were thousands of crosses of Americans who died in World War II. It was beautifully kept, every blade of grass cut, and every path neat and clean.

Claiborne recalled the war memorial he had seen on Corregidor where the inscription read: "Sleep my sons your duty is done for freedom's right has come. Sleep in the silent depths of the sea or in your bed of hallowed sod until you hear at dawn the low, clear reveille of God." It was an awe-inspiring monument that touched the soul.

The chartered Boeing 707 flew the group into Tan Son Nhut airport on Tuesday, February 25, and they were quickly loaded on two heavily armored military busses. Jeep-loads of American MPs and a contingent of Vietnamese police with sirens screaming raced through rush hour traffic to the Caravelle Hotel. American soldiers surrounded the hotel and security guards monitored everyone. "We just blasted through there," Claiborne said.

After a brief rest, the travelers climbed back on the army busses and were briefed by General Creighton Abrams at his headquarters on the air base. It was a grim and candid briefing that left the businessmen in a somber mood when the busses sped back to the Caravelle.

The beautiful old hotel had begun to show wartime wear and tear, but the travelers were entertained on the roof garden that evening. Cocktails were served by waiters in white coats, and the garden was festooned with flowers. In the distance they could hear rumbling booms as the B-52s hit their targets ten miles away. Flares shone brilliantly in the distance. "Nobody seemed to worry about it, so we got used to it," said Claiborne.

After dinner with the Saigon press corps the travelers gradually faded away to their rooms, a bit apprehensive about their quarters. The day before, two Communist rockets fell just two blocks from the hotel.

"My room was on the second floor," said Claiborne, "and my first thought was this was not really kept up. I killed a big roach in the bathroom. Then I thought that if a bomb hits out in the street, it will impact on the first and second floors." Though he was uneasy, the night passed without incident.

According to a *Time* report of the tour, the businessmen were dressed in green army fatigues and combat boots, and left at 5:30 a.m. for the Tan Son Nhut airbase in the armored military busses. They boarded a C-130 troop carrier piloted by Major General Burl McLaughlin, chief of army air transport in Vietnam, who claimed that he ran the world's busiest and largest airline. The general throttled the C-130 into "a fighter-like takeoff to gain as much altitude as he could in the shortest possible time. This was a week of a new enemy offensive, and he was carrying an unusual cargo."

First they stopped at Cam Ranh Bay air base to view the planes flown in Vietnam. Then they were strapped into floatable flack vests and helmets and hustled onto boats to watch a naval fire power demonstration in the South China Sea. Later they were flown in the C-130 to Pleiku to be briefed. The military told the group that the U.S. could win the war in a week if permitted to do so, but that an all-out effort remained a political decision.

Claiborne and others expressed frustration at the inability for prompt military action. Helicopters waited to take the businessmen to various sites of interest. "The three hour helicopter tour — and stops — more than anything else, gave the tour the sights, sounds, smell, and dusty feel of Vietnam as a country at war," said the *Time* report.

The C-130, with General McLaughlin at the controls, took the group back to Saigon for a reception at the home of U.S. Ambassador Elsworth Bunker. By the end of what one businessman described as the most thrilling day of his life, the group was exhausted.

The next day, the businessmen had an audience with President Nguyen Van Thieu at the presidential palace, followed by a Chinese meal in the dining room. Shark fin soup, Pigeon duck (sic), and a Vietnamese brandy were served, and the businessmen were relaxed as they boarded busses for the flight to Bangkok.

In Thailand they visited the king's 50-acre estate in the heart of Bangkok, where the king managed to talk Jim Linen, CEO of TIME, Inc., into a gift of two schoolhouses, instead of one. Then they were off to Malaysia, where they had tea with the prime minister at the banquet hall next to his residence. There the talk was on economics, the war in Vietnam, and regional independence.

On March 1, they touched down in Singapore for a luncheon and briefing by Prime Minister Lee Kuan Yew. He predicted the U.S. would lose the war in America, not in Vietnam, suggesting the lack of a national will to win. The group then moved on to the Hotel Indonesia in Djakarta, where they were briefed at the American embassy and attended a dinner where the speaker was Foreign Minister Adam Malik.

In Seoul, Korea, on March 4, President Chung Hee Park entertained them in the presidential residence. Later they were bundled up in fur-collared parkas and old fashioned G.I. issue galoshes and taken in Huey choppers to the Demilitarized Zone, complete with a tour of an observation post and meal of fried chicken at the G.I. mess hall. In downtown Seoul, they met for a briefing with the American ambassador for a discussion of the military and economic picture.

The last stop was Japan. On March 5, they moved to the Miyako Hotel in Kyoto for a discussion with a panel of Japanese intellectuals about culture, and on the 6th went on to the Okura Hotel in Tokyo to speak with a panel of Japan's top businessmen about trade. Premier Eisaku Sato met them at a reception given by Japanese Foreign Minister Kiichji Aichi at the Hotel New Otani in Tokyo.

Claiborne was impressed by the courtesy of the Japanese people. With some friends, he went down to the Ginza for shopping. They were to meet their driver at 5 p.m., but he did not appear. They tried to flag a taxi in the rush hour traffic, but with no success. At 6 p.m. they were beginning to get a bit uneasy, because a 7:00 dinner was scheduled at the hotel.

Suddenly, an expensive car with a chauffeur pulled up and a Japanese gentleman asked in perfect English, "Can I be of any help?" Relieved, the travelers explained that they had be back at the Okura Hotel. "He took us to the hotel and was most gracious," said Claiborne. "That was a wonderful experience." They returned to the United States from Tokyo, arriving in San Francisco at 2 a.m. March 8.

The remarkable experience of the *Time* trips, with the information he learned, the places he visited, and the friends he made, remained a treasured memory for Claiborne. The magazine also invited him to what he terms, "the most remarkable dinner I ever attended."

The event was *Time* magazine's 40th anniversary in 1963, and

Claiborne and Lora were invited. Publisher Henry R. Luce hosted the dinner attended by nearly 300 of the men and women who had appeared on *Time* covers since 1923. Claiborne and Lora joined *Time* executives and major advertisers at New York's Waldorf-Astoria Hotel on May 6. The celebrities and guests gathered in the hotel's Starlight Room at elegant tables under magnificent chandeliers.

"That was one of the most interesting evenings that we ever had — my wife and I were so privileged," remembered Claiborne. "They say there has never been such an array of celebrities in one ballroom in the country before or since as there was that night. Apparently everybody, or virtually everybody they had asked had come and they had come from all over the world. You had heads of state, you had presidents, you had vice presidents, you had prime ministers. We had a scientist who had won Nobel prizes. We had movie actresses and actors. We had boxers: Jack Dempsey and Joe Lewis. Joe DiMaggio was there. Any number of famous sports figures were there. I have never been someone to walk a block to see someone who might be passing through, but I was impressed with this group of people. I remember Gina Lollobrigida; I don't know why I remember that," he laughed.

"We were advertising in *Time* magazine and so they had 40 or 50 of their leading advertisers. We were one of their better advertisers at one time."

Claiborne and Lora were seated next to Conrad Hilton, owner of the Waldorf. "Our tables were assigned," recalled Claiborne. "There was a couple sitting there, an older gentleman and a very sweet young thing across from him — obviously his date — and so I introduced myself, and he said, 'I'm Conrad Hilton.' And of course Conrad Hilton owned the Waldorf where this was being held. And I don't know why I foolishly said, 'Well we'll have a good dinner tonight.'"

Time's covers included boxers Jack Demsey, Gene Tunney and Joe Lewis; baseball stars George Sisler, Bob Feller, Jackie Robinson and Casey Stengel; tennis champions Don Budge, Jack

Kramer, Dick Savitt, and Althea Gibson; and football greats Sam Huff, Vince Lombardi and Bobby Layne.

Theater and movie stars and famed musicians included Helen Hayes, Bette Davis, Ginger Rogers, Ethel Merman, Judith Anderson, Ruth Gordon, Bob Hope, Joan Fontaine, Jennifer Jones, Danny Kaye, Marian Anderson, Olivia de Havilland, Milton Berle, Margot Fonteyn, Carol Channing, Patrice Munsel, Gina Lollobrigida, Gwen Verdon, Dave Brubeck, Rex Harrison, Jack Paar, Harry Belafonte, Richard Boone, Leotine Price, Edgar Bergen, Billy Rose, Mort Sahl, Rosalind Russell, Ed Sullivan, Robert Preston, and Ina Claire.

Authors included John Dos Passos, Morris Fishbein, Hedda Hopper, Mortimer J. Adler, Herman Wouk, John Gunther, James Reston, and Jean Kerr.

Also present were chief executive officers representing 28 major corporations, including Coca Cola, CBS, NBC, Chrysler Corp., General Electric, General Motors, Ford Motor, Pan American World Airways, Chase Manhattan Bank, Mellon National Bank, Eastern Airlines, E. I. Dupont, RCA, Westinghouse, IBM, New York Stock Exchange, and Procter and Gamble.

U.S. Army generals present were Omar Bradley, Douglas MacArthur, Lucius D. Clay, Matthew B. Ridgeway, James VanFleet, Mark W. Clark, Lauris Norstad, Lyman L. Lemnitzer and Maxwell D. Taylor. Navy admirals were Emory S. Land, Arthur W. Radford, Arleigh A. Burke. Air Force generals in attendance were James H. Doolittle, Ira C. Eaker, Carl Spaatz, Nathan F. Twining, and Thomas D. White.

Present and former U.S. senators included Claude Pepper, Florida; Leverett Saltonstall, Massachusetts; W. Stuart Symington, Missouri; Estes Kefauver, Tennessee, John Sherman Cooper, Kentucky; Clifford Case, New Jersey; Hubert H. Humphrey, Minnesota; Margaret Chase Smith, Maine; Barry Goldwater, Arizona; Everette M. Dirksen, Illinois, Burton K. Wheeler, Montana; and Ernest Gruening, Alaska.

Closer to home, Claiborne's friend, the Reverend Dr. Theodore F. Adams, of First Baptist Church in Richmond, was there. He had been on the cover of *Time* December 5, 1955 as President of the Baptist World Alliance. Other government and religious leaders, foreign leaders, scientists and artists also attended the dinner.

Reminiscing on these trips, Claiborne relished the experiences that provided him a greater scope in world affairs. Grateful for the exposure, Claiborne reciprocated by always leaving a good impression of himself, his company and his hometown of Richmond, Virginia.

XI

PHILANTHROPY

The December 1983 issue of *Town & Country* included an article entitled, "The Most Generous Living Americans," with E. Claiborne Robins listed in the top five. At that time he had given away over $100 million. The joy of giving has long been one of Claiborne's most gratifying personal quests, and his gifts have reached thousands of grateful recipients. The wealth he amassed through the stock market and company profits provided not only prosperity for his family, but the means for Claiborne to pay back the good fortune that had blessed his life.

"Betty has added up that over the past 30 years I have contributed over $250 million," said Claiborne, referring to Betty Brown, his executive assistant. "I think that's a figure that we ought to use because while I may have contributed over $250 million, I think it is a more conservative estimate.

"It has always been my philosophy — not that you do it for this means — but most of the things that you do in this world come back to you in the form of blessings of various kinds, and certainly I have been very blessed in so many ways. I think everything I have ever given away has come back to me.

"I've always had the philosophy that I try to give back to the community and to the country, hopefully, a good bit of what I earn, and I have done so many years. Right now, I give away over 50 percent of what comes in. I don't need but so much to eat and live. I made two gifts as of yesterday totaling $750,000," he said in a 1992 interview.

There is little doubt that Claiborne's great gifts to the University of Richmond, his alma mater, will be his most widely remembered philanthropic contributions. This is true not only because of the huge amount of money involved, but because of the thousands of people whose lives it affected. Every student who walks away with a degree from the University of Richmond also carries with it a debt of gratitude to Claiborne Robins and his family.

The transformation of a small, struggling, Baptist institution into a strong, independent university ranking on a national level began in an almost casual way. Claiborne, who had been named to the Board of Trustees of the University of Richmond, soon became a member of the executive committee. At a meeting in the spring of 1969, President George M. Modlin outlined to his committee the growing needs of the university, and they were many.

"The University of Richmond was solid financially, thanks to the tightfisted budgeting efforts of treasurer Charles Wheeler," explained Claiborne, "but the university was struggling."

Claiborne thought long and hard about his loyalty to the school and his commitment to higher education and his community. Then he asked the question that changed the lives of thousands: "George, how much would it take to put us on a firm foundation?"

Dr. Modlin thought for a minute and then replied, "That's difficult to answer, but about $50 million."

That afternoon, as he drove back to his office, Claiborne considered making a gift to the university, a gift large enough to solve the university's most severe problems, put it on a solid financial footing, and encourage others to join the cause.

His business and social peers in Richmond and other parts of Virginia had often annoyed him with their insistence that the University of Virginia was THE university in Virginia. They made it clear that UR was considered a small Baptist school with little or no impact on Richmond or the state, and certainly not the nation.

Would an initial gift of $20 million be enough? No. Claiborne thought that even the $50 million that Dr. Modlin had estimated would not be enough to do the job. If he was to be successful in starting the University of Richmond on the road to national prominence, his gift would have to be spectacular, perhaps totaling the $50 million Dr. Modlin had suggested.

Back at his office, Claiborne called in his tax and legal experts and explored the question. Could he do it? Yes, but how would it be structured? The decision was made quickly. Claiborne's gift would be $50 million, but $10 million of that would be in a challenge grant, matching a dollar for every dollar raised from other gifts. The matching feature was particularly important, Claiborne thought, because it would encourage others to give to the university.

Claiborne made up his mind, and his gift to the university excited the academic world. At the time, this was the largest gift by one family to a private university in the history of the United States. The news of the gift, and the expanded goals for the university, created challenges and excitement on the part of the faculty and administration.

The gift also distanced the university from religious ties, something Claiborne decided was essential to the school.

"One stipulation at the time of the major gift, was that the Baptists would not control the institution," explained Claiborne. "They had to give up control before I made the gift. I think that was one of the greatest things I ever did for the university, besides the gift."

Dr. Modlin, under whose stewardship the university had maintained an academic respectability while struggling financially, decided to step aside as president to let new leadership move the university forward. A search committee screened a number of prospective candidates and finally settled on the young president of Meredith College in Raleigh, North Carolina as their first choice.

Dr. E. Bruce Heilman, a slender Kentuckian with a friendly and effective style, had impressed the committee with his vision and his no-nonsense approach to university leadership. His philosophy was identical to that of Claiborne's: A university must have money and lots of it to provide the resources needed to achieve greatness.

Reluctant at first to take the presidency, Dr. Heilman reconsidered after discussing with Claiborne his vision of the university's future. "Claiborne Robins not only laid $50 million on the table," recalled Dr. Heilman, "he also put up his heart, mind and energy."

Though he was as busy as usual, Claiborne somehow found time for University of Richmond appointments. Dr. Heilman had hardly settled in Richmond when Claiborne sponsored a joint reception at the Commonwealth Club for Dr. Heilman and Ken Roberts, the new president of Central National Bank. Dr. Heilman had an instant introduction to Richmond's business and social community.

Claiborne believed in Bruce Heilman, and the two executives became good friends. While the pressure was sometimes intense for Claiborne to settle disputes at the University of Richmond, as

Claiborne speaks at the Robins Center at the University of Richmond on the occasion of the Robins Center Dedication, February 24, 1973, with Ann Carol, Lora and Claiborne Jr. Photos courtesy of the University of Richmond.

its largest benefactor, he steadfastly refused to interfere with decisions made by the president.

At one point, the question arose as to whether or not the football coach should continue to be the athletic director, as was the case when Dr. Heilman took office. Dr. Heilman's perception was that the two responsibilities should be separated. When that decision impacted on the university's athletic alumni and other supporters, it caused some turmoil in the university ranks and even in the local press.

Quietly, Claiborne let his view be known: the president of the university makes the decisions and the board of trustees either supports those decisions or gets another president. Dr. Heilman called a special board meeting to deal with the situation. His decision was upheld.

"He created a comfort zone," Dr. Heilman said of Claiborne. "It was a comfortable friendship that developed over time. He laid out his vision in general terms and, from time to time, he and I would talk about it and interpret it. Putting my father aside, I couldn't respect any man more than I respect Claiborne Robins. I also have a great respect for Mrs. Robins."

Claiborne's interest in athletics spurred another gift to the university. During the middle 1960s, Claiborne had asked his children to put aside some money earmarked for building a new athletic facility at the University of Richmond. They joined him in his vision of a place where the university's basketball games would be played on the campus. In 1969 the pool of money raised by the family for the athletic center had reached $4.5 million.

"Dr. Modlin invited me over for the bid opening," said Claiborne Jr., who represented the family. "The first bid opened was $10.7 million. The next was $11.3 million and the third bid was $12.8 million. I called Dad and told him what the bids were and he got the family together and said that we had to decide whether or not to go on with the project or drop it. Of course we decided to go ahead," said Claiborne Jr.

The beginning of Claiborne's generosity to the University of Richmond was in 1947 when Dr. Modlin called on Claiborne to serve on a fund-raising committee. Claiborne, busy building the A. H. Robins Company, had already scheduled every minute of his time and apologized for refusing to help, but he gave Dr. Modlin a check for $5,000.

Claiborne would never refuse the university his generosity, and a long string of gifts changed the face of the campus and elevated the quality of the school. Robins Memorial Field was dedicated in

Lora Robins Court Dedication
Spring, 1980
Family portrait, left to right: Robert Porter,
Betty Porter, Claiborne Robins, Lora Robins,
Juliet Shield, Ann Carol Haskell, Mary Ellen
Robins and Claiborne Robins, Jr. At right,
Claiborne enjoys the luncheon. Photos courtesy
of the University of Richmond.

1953, Robins Hall in 1959, the $50 million challenge was given in 1969, the president's home in 1972, the Robins Center in 1972, Lora Robins Gallery in 1977, the E. Claiborne Robins School of Business in 1979, and the Lora Robins Court in 1980.

Harder to find on this list, but very significant in the total, are the continuing gifts of money, most unheralded, but given freely because of some unforeseen need or ongoing project at UR. In all, Claiborne and his family have given the University of Richmond more than $100 million.

Claiborne's benevolence helped the University of Richmond rank among the leaders in private institutions in the nation, and Claiborne delights in its prominence today.

"It's been so exciting to watch the development that has occurred to the university since the gift was made. The changes have been enormous, not only in the buildings, of course, which were necessary, but in the quality of the teaching, in the beauty of the grounds, all of the things which go into making a great educational institution," said Claiborne.

"We are moving fast, getting good people on the board. We are getting a fairly wealthy clientele. Some are children of prominent people who have some means, some people who have the ability to make it great. You cannot have a great institution without having the funds to make it great. You must have the teachers, make the campus attractive, buildings up-to-date, and so on. It takes a lot of money.

"I have no hesitation in saying that the university in the next 20 years will be considered one of the five or six premier institutions in the country. It may come sooner than I think, because even we don't realize how its fame is spreading."

Even greater than his loyalty to the University of Richmond, however, Claiborne's reasons for giving so generously are founded in his deeply held respect and enduring commitment to education.

"I've always believed that education is the greatest investment that any individual or corporation or foundation could

Claiborne and Lora at a University of Richmond function in the late 1980s.

possibly make," he said. "It is something that has an impact not only on the present generation but on many, many generations to come. I can't think of any other type of giving with so significant an impact on society.

"As I was casting about to decide where to make the greatest impact, I felt that the University of Richmond had the greatest opportunity for outstanding success. The university was a good university to begin with. It had one of the most beautiful campuses in the United States. It had a good faculty. It had many of the things which go to make up an outstanding university, but it lacked the one thing which was essential to be a great university, and that is enough resources to accomplish this goal.

"I could see with the firm foundation that existed at the University of Richmond there was a tremendous opportunity here for anyone who made a significant gift to have a terrific impact, and it's turned out to be the case.

"You know it is one of the mysteries of life to me that so many folks wait until they die to do what they really wanted to do all along, such as a large gift to a university. I think the fact that my family and I did it when we did it has made it very exciting for all of us because we've been able to see with our own eyes the tremendous accomplishments of the University of Richmond.

"I know it is better to give in your will than not give at all, but I can tell anyone from personal experience that you'll get a hundred times the satisfaction of doing it while you are alive.

"If I had waited to give this money until my death, say in a couple of years from now, the University of Richmond might have gone under in the meantime. I hope my children have seen this vision. Don't wait until next week, or next month, you may not be alive by then. I'm not a pessimist, I'm a realist. If you want to do something, do it. That's my philosophy."

Claiborne (third from left) with former University of Richmond presidents Dr. E. Bruce Heilman and Dr. George M. Modlin, and current president Dr. Richard L. Morrill on June 9, 1994.

Claiborne's obvious pleasure in giving for educational causes was not limited to the University of Richmond. One of the historic moments in his life came in 1981, when he was called upon to help save Virginia Union University, a predominantly black institution in Richmond.

The university, due for an accreditation examination, was so badly in debt that it would have not met the minimum standards. Claiborne joined Tennant Bryan of Richmond Newspapers,

James Wheat of Wheat, First Securities, and Sydney Lewis of Best Products company in heading up the rescue effort. In a series of quick phone calls the four business leaders arranged a meeting of 60 civic leaders. The message was clear.

"Virginia Union is facing a disaster," Claiborne explained. "We need to raise $750,000 in 45 days, and it has to be in cash, not pledges. We each got up and stated why the university was important to our community. In that one meeting we got over $750,000, paid within the next ten days. Virginia Union University got the accreditation and from that point they went uphill. They got a new president, they got fiscal control, they got new accountants to keep things in order and as a result they are in far stronger shape today."

Again, Claiborne's highly placed value for education prompted his championing of Virginia Union. "Education is the salvation if there is any solution to the problems in our society," said Claiborne. "Education is the most important thing. If we could get more people who are uneducated educated, there would be less poverty, there would be less crime. I can't think of anything that is more important for success and more important for a happy life than a good education."

Orchestrating the fund drive for Virginia Union University, Claiborne learned that a strong leadership role is essential for success, and that a good example can foster even greater community generosity.

"To be able to go to the business community and say in effect we want $750,000 cash in ten days — that's no small feat," he said. "I think it was because of the four men that were there. I'm sure that if you got four other individuals who didn't have the respect and admiration that apparently we did, ... I don't think we'd have been able to do it.

"Top people have to be involved in any campaign if it is to succeed. I've been a fund-raiser for many organizations, either heading a drive or contributing. I headed a drive for Hampton

Institute one year, one of the wealthiest institutions in Virginia. Over the years I've asked many important people in Richmond for money.

"That has one drawback," he laughed. "When they come back to see you later on for their causes, well, you feel obligated to give and, of course, you do. There is a lot of give and take. When you are raising money of any size, you have to have people with some clout. If you can get somebody with clout to head the drive ... a lot depends on who it is and the influence in the community."

Claiborne's influence in Richmond was considerable, and not only for enlisting donors to causes he espoused. By giving large sums, Claiborne inspired others to give with equal magnanimity to their own causes.

"I have been told by alumni of other colleges in the state, ... none of whom knew the other that had told me this. I have been told by leading alumni of VMI, Washington and Lee, Randolph Macon, Hampton Sydney, University of Virginia, William and Mary, and perhaps some others that I haven't thought of, that I triggered their campaigns and enabled them to raise, collectively, hundreds of millions of dollars that they would not have been able to raise if it had not been for ... it really is gratifying.

"In a way, they are competitors," he chuckled. "You have a little mixed emotion there, but on the other hand, it's a very wonderful thing to think that one gift should have inspired so many. Elmon Gray told me that VMI had a campaign to raise $50 million. VMI is a rather small school. He told me that they would never have achieved their goal had it not been for my gift, which I thought was a very generous statement, but very satisfying, and he was very sincere, I think, when he said that."

Claiborne's success in giving defines the philanthropy that also spread throughout his company and friends. Many people in need became recipients of Claiborne's financial support. When asked once if he had applied the golden rule to employees and done anything above and beyond for his friends, he was quick to answer.

"I could almost fill you a book," said Claiborne. "I won't mention any names. These are things that are being said for the first time. Nobody knows about this except my secretary. I doubt if even my family knows about it because I didn't feel it was the sort of thing to make public.

"There was one young lady whose husband left her with a small child, and he was a despicable scoundrel. She tried to get child support. He remarried; he never did give her any child support. She was in desperate circumstances. I made her several gifts over a period of five years to keep her afloat.

"There was another gentleman who developed a brain tumor, and he wanted to go to a very prominent physician in California because he had heard that he was one of the best in the country, and he had met him personally when he was in the service, and I heard about it, and I knew that he was making fair money, but he didn't have really a lot of money to spare. So I gave him money to go to California to have that brain tumor operation. He came through it fine and is still living today.

"There was another gentleman, one of our scientific people. He had a very tragic situation. He had a place down on the river that he just loved, and he lived down there every waking moment that he wasn't actually in Richmond. One of the hurricane storm's high tides came in and just practically devastated it, ruined all of his furniture and did about $15,000 or $20,000 worth of damage to his home. I knew what the home meant to him, so I gave him $10,000 and loaned him $5,000. The reason for that strange division was I felt he would feel a little more comfortable having something to pay back.

"There were several people that I gave money to to make a down payment on a home because I knew them. I made a loan to one of our black employees. I heard he had a 12 percent bank loan that was eating him alive. I said to him one day, 'There's no reason for you to pay 12 percent. I'll loan you the money at 6 percent and you pay off that other loan.' So he did that, and I gave him the money to pay off the loan and to make this purchase, and he's paid off every penny of it. It took him awhile, but he's paid it off.

"There are several folks — one of the folks that I used to do business with — he was in the real estate business and he always looked after my interests. He died and his wife was in pretty bad shape financially. He hadn't saved very much, and I helped her out several times over a period.

"Then there were a couple of friends that we knew that were struggling and we helped them some .... As I say, nobody knows about any of these things. I don't know whether I want to put too much in the book. Some of them I found out through Betty Brown. Some of them I found out through my own knowledge of the situation.

"There was a fine young man who I liked very much who got into a problem with alcohol and got very down, was separated, and he literally had nobody to help him out. I got somebody to act as a trustee for the money, and I gave him some money to keep him afloat, but I didn't give it to him directly because it might have gone for alcohol, but they kept an eye on it and dispersed it to him when he needed it. I probably saved his life.

"Do you remember this former postman, this fellow in Richmond who gets publicity every now and then, the postman who gives away $1,000 to worthy people and to worthy causes? Well, one time I heard that his wife was not in too good shape, so I sat down and wrote him a check for $2,000 and said, 'You have been so good to others that I think it's time that you will receive it.' And I only put one stipulation on this check," he laughed. "'Don't you give it away right away.' I heard from him, of course, and he was most appreciative.

"I never have been one to loan money too much, except to people that I knew were struggling and that if I didn't get it back I wouldn't worry. The amazing thing — with one exception over my entire lifetime — they always paid me back.

"One of them was a friend of mine who was in the printing business, and I guess I shouldn't identify the business because that might show who it was. But I knew his situation, I knew how honest he was, and due to a series of circumstances beyond his control, he needed a lot of money, and I loaned it to him. That's the only big loan I ever made, and he paid it back with interest, every bit of it with interest."

Claiborne's personal interest in helping good causes spanned many races and religions. "The Catholics say I'm one of their best supporters and the Jews say I'm one of their best supporters," he laughed. It was true in both cases. Claiborne supported as many worthwhile causes over the years as possible.

Claiborne was proud of his association with the Alec de Toqueville Society, a group of the leading contributors to the United Way, people who give at least $10,000 or more personally each year. The society includes 65 to 70 of the top givers in Richmond and was formed by Ric Deane.

In 1992 the society presented Claiborne with an award which included two bound volumes of de Toqueville's "Democracy in America." Alexis de Toqueville was a Frenchman who recognized the greatness of democracy in America and wrote about how it works and how it differs from other countries. He stressed how private philanthropy could make a great impact on society, a message that hit home for Claiborne.

Unfortunately, Claiborne has realized, the value of giving is not broadly recognized. "The de Toqueville Society is composed of about 70 members, more or less," he said. "If I took those 70 people and any worthy cause, it would probably be the same people on the list of donors to that cause," he said.

"It's tragic that so many people of means have not discovered the joy of giving. That may sound like a platitude, but it's so true. You have to give. You don't know how satisfying it is until you have done it."

XII

THE DALKON SHIELD

In the 1960s women welcomed birth control choices that gave them freedom from compulsory motherhood. Both oral contraceptives and intrauterine devices [IUDs] gained in use. However, when both the scientific and popular press began publishing articles that questioned the safety of the Pill, scaring the millions of American women taking it, a Senate sub-committee on oral contraceptives convened in 1970 in order to clear up the confusion.

When the hearings closed, the subcommitte concluded that the risks of taking oral contraceptives predominated over the benefits, and alternative methods of contraception were considered. As a result, IUDs gained in popularity and were soon promoted by groups like the Population Council as the preferred birth control method for family planning in the U.S. and in underdeveloped countries.

A. H. Robins became interested in IUDs when it learned of a new device — the Dalkon Shield — developed by Dr. Hugh J. Davis, assistant professor of obstetrics and gynecology at the prestigious Johns Hopkins University in Baltimore. According to Dr. Davis, in 1969 the Dalkon Shield had been tested with promising results. He reported a 1.1 percent pregnancy rate based on 640 insertions. This rate was considerably lower than any competing IUD.

After a bidding rivalry with the Upjohn Company, A. H. Robins acquired the patent from the Dalkon Corporation — in part owned by Dr. Davis — for $750,000 in 1970. Labeled by the FDA as a medical device, the Dalkon Shield did not require FDA approval and after making a few refinements to the Shield, A. H. Robins began marketing the IUD six months later. The Dalkon

Shield cost 37 cents to produce and retailed at $4.35, making it a potentially lucrative acquisition.

"It seemed like such a coup," wrote *The Commonwealth* magazine in a feature article on A. H. Robins in June 1982. "It had beaten the Upjohn Company to the product by a hair's breadth, and it wasn't long before Robins had captured 40 percent of the IUD market .... Then, suddenly the acquisition that had seemed as magical as Cinderella's slipper became an Achilles' heel."

Rather than a financial boon, the Dalkon Shield put Robins in sudden peril. Within a few years of acquiring the Dalkon patent, the company and its insurance carrier would be forced to pay millions in settlement of cases filed by those who claimed the device had caused infection, pregnancy, septic abortion, sterility, perforation of the uterus, even death.

In June 1974, the FDA requested that Robins stop marketing the Dalkon Shield until its safety could be reviewed. With peak sales of more than 3 million Dalkon Shields in the U.S. and abroad, and the number of suits being brought against the company increasing, A. H. Robins halted sales of the product.

In August 1974, the FDA Drug and Device panels were convened into an 18 member panel, known as the Ad Hoc Committee which held 13 hours of public hearings on the Dalkon Shield. The following month a subcommittee of the original panel met and drafted a report concluding that, "It is not apparent that the safety and efficacy of the Dalkon Shield is significantly different from other IUDs."

By December 1974, FDA Commissioner Alexander Schmidt announced that Robins could resume distribution of the Shield, but only under the controlled conditions of a registry system. However, with the number of cases mounting, and the adverse publicity the Shield was receiving, A. H. Robins decided not to resume marketing the device.

During this time period, company stock, which had sold for

$40.75 a share in 1973, plummeted. The high in 1974 was $25.50; in 1975, $15.75, and in 1976, $12.75.

In one of the largest settlements of its time, a Denver jury in 1979 awarded $6.8 million to a woman who had claimed to be injured by the Dalkon Shield. The decision was promptly appealed by the company. With that award, A. H. Robins stock hit an all-time low of $6.62, well below the then current book value of $9.04.

During 1970 Claiborne became chairman of the board, relinquishing some of his day to day duties to his President, William Zimmer. In 1975 William Zimmer retired, and Claiborne stepped down as chief executive officer. As the new President and CEO, Claiborne Jr. guided the company through the end of the 1970s and into the decade of the 1980s with the mounting problems of the Dalkon Shield lurking in the background. By August 1985, the claims paid had amounted to more than $378 million, with another $107 million going to legal fees.

A. H. Robins asked the protection of the bankruptcy court in August 1985 and continued to operate under Chapter 11 of the bankruptcy laws. Overall company sales continued to increase while a resolution of the situation unfolded in the courts. Three plans of reorganization failed, but the fourth, filed with the bankruptcy court in February of 1988, was workable.

In December of 1989, A. H. Robins Company was sold to American Home Products, a multi-national corporation and maker of prescription and over-the-counter drugs. Under the agreement, and as stipulated by the Robins reorganization plan, $2.5 billion was paid to two trusts to satisfy Dalkon Shield claims, and Robins stockholders received stock worth approximately $900 million. Although it was painful for the family to sell the company founded by Albert Hartley Robins, the price was excellent.

A. H. Robins could not have predicted in the '70s what was to happen in the future. The company thought it had purchased an outstanding product, based on the information provided by Dr. Davis. With the concern about the increase in world population, the IUD was considered to be an acceptable device, with acceptable side effects, supported by numerous organizations. In addition, in the early '70s medical devices did not require FDA approval prior to their introduction to the market. Only when problems became apparent were defective products removed from the market by the FDA.

For A. H. Robins there were no warning signs, no previous model for them to follow, no comparable product liability cases in either the legal or medical fields, and given the litigious nature of the '80s the company faced unprecedented legal action.

Claiborne was stung by accusations made by plaintiff attorneys in the court battles. Moreover, he felt the media was too eager to place blame on the company by publishing and airing pieces biased against the company, with reports that were either inaccurate or incomplete. Claiborne Jr., as quoted in the August 1, 1984 issue of the *New York Times* said, "Why doesn't the American public realize that a company that is over 100 years old wouldn't make a decision that could destroy it in a matter of minutes?"

The negative allegations and resulting publicity delivered a severe blow to Claiborne, a man who had devoted his life to helping others achieve a better life, and whose greatest pleasure was in seeing the millions of dollars he had given to others generate a higher level of prosperity and happiness.

"The Dalkon Shield not only took its toll on stock, but on the Robins family and the work force as well," reported *Commonwealth*. The magazine quoted someone close to the company as saying, 'The Dalkon Shield was a terrible trauma. He (Claiborne) felt they had been producing quality products for years. It hurt him because it hurt his people and hurt the company's image.'"

Claiborne's greatest sorrow at the loss of the company was a feeling that he was being forced to leave his extended family. He realized that his personal approach with employees could never be duplicated by new management.

The experience was particularly distasteful for Claiborne as evidence surfaced in later years that stated that the Dalkon Shield was as good as any intrauterine device marketed in the early 1970s. "Two papers just recently published," Claiborne said in 1992, "that say that the Dalkon Shield was as safe as any on the market at that time and that the studies used against us were badly flawed and they point out in these studies where they were flawed. One of the papers that Claiborne was referring to is, "The Intrauterine Device and Pelvic Inflammatory Disease: The Women's Health Study Reanalyzed," published in 1991 in the *Journal of Clinical Epidemiology*.

Claiborne continued, "They went on to cite that so many cases brought against the Dalkon Shield were from pelvic inflammatory disease that were supposedly caused by the Dalkon Shield. They point out the percentage of women who have this problem who have never used any contraceptive. But, of course, everybody that got a pelvic infection automatically went to the Dalkon Shield. There is no evidence, credible evidence, that the Dalkon Shield was faulty or that it was inferior or not as good as any other.

"They pointed out that the knowledge of the physicians in inserting this had a great deal to do with effectiveness and lack of problems. Physicians who were knowledgeable and had inserted hundreds and hundreds never had any problems at all," Claiborne said.

"I felt all along that we were on the side of right despite the attempt of lawyers to make of us a very dark case," Claiborne maintained. "And having faith in the Lord that things were going to come out all right sort of enabled us to pull through this very trying period. It turned out pretty well," he said speaking from a businessman's point of view. "We did have to sell the company, but we got a good price for it."

Concern over the curse of litigation remains a sore point for Claiborne, who criticizes the legal system for encouraging unscrupulous law practices.

Claiborne remembers Lee Iacocca as saying, 'One reason the Japanese are so far ahead of us is that they have as many lawyers in Japan as we have sumo wrestlers in this country.' Every business that operates has a built-in cost, an enormous cost that you have to pass on because of litigation.

"If the average individual knew how much the cost of litigation is in the price of every product they buy ... There is not a thing that you and I buy that isn't more expensive because of litigation, because there isn't any company that I know of, of any size, that doesn't have numerous cases of litigation of one kind or another.

"There ought to be a ceiling or cap. No jury should be able to award a huge amount just because they think a firm has deep pockets. In Canada, no jury is allowed to award judgments with things of a scientific nature, because they aren't qualified.

"So, we saw the evidence of having the great abuse of the legal system. Cases were drummed up by the lawyers. They'd advertise for clients: 'Have you ever used the Dalkon Shield?' They didn't say have you ever been injured by it? Have you ever used it? That's all they wanted. They took full advantage and it was a very ghastly experience."

Still, Claiborne's respect for individuals within the legal system remained unchanged. He recalled attending a dinner meeting in a recent year where he was seated next to Judge Mehrige, who officiated over the Dalkon Shield hearing.

"I've always admired Judge Mehrige as being a tough but fair individual, and I was told by folks who heard him say this after the meeting: I was told that Judge Mehrige frequently said that one of the nicest things that had happened to him in some time was the privilege of sitting by me.

"I was very touched," said Claiborne. "(His) remark just stunned me. The lawyers had tried their best to make a case that we were best friends with the judge and that he was biased. Actually, I have never invited Judge Mehrige to our home and I have never been in his home, socially. They couldn't make a very good case. We had no real friendship other than being neighbors. I admired his fairness and integrity," Claiborne said.

In the final days before the settlement Claiborne Jr. told his father that he felt that the company could be saved by borrowing heavily. Claiborne thought about it and finally turned to Claiborne Jr. and replied: "Son, we have gone as far as our leadership can take us. It is now time to turn it over to someone else."

Claiborne Jr. said later, "That piece of advice, as I look back upon it today, was the best he had given me in my entire career."

In retrospect, Claiborne viewed the Dalkon debacle as a crucible in his later life and a hurdle he overcame with his usual optimism. "He never looked back," said Claiborne Jr. "He said that there's nothing you can do about what's gone by, but you can always do something about what's ahead of you."

"I could cite several instances in my life when things looked kind of dark at the moment," explained Claiborne, "but if you have faith that things are going to turn out all right, they usually do. There are very few things that turn out as bad as you think they are going to. It's true that you think that at the time, that it is life's darkest moment, but you look back on it years later and think that it was one of the best things that ever happened to you.

"In the first place," said Claiborne, "I'm an optimistic person by nature. I've never been a pessimist. Betty Brown said when all this Dalkon stuff was going on, I'd come in smiling just like I always did. I felt that it was going to work out all right because I knew that we were in the right, that all this stuff that was going on was not what should be going on, and that I didn't deserve anything but a favorable outcome, and it worked out that way.

XIII

Life After A. H. Robins

After the sale of the A. H. Robins Company in December 1989, Claiborne adjusted his life, toning down from the hectic business schedule he had followed for decades in respect for the natural constraints of age.

"There is one thing about old Mother Nature," Claiborne remarked. "Mother Nature has a way of telling you what you can do and what you can't do. Because of my limited physical abilities, I don't have a lot of choice," he chuckled. "I've got to stay busy doing something, and thanks to Mother Nature, I have discovered what my schedule should be.

"What I do is that I arise around 6 a.m., I read the morning paper, and watch the morning news on television. I usually fix the breakfast because I'm up early, and breakfast is a very simple thing. Even I can fix breakfast. So I fix the breakfast, and when it's ready I call my wife and she comes down about 7:30."

Even in retirement, however, Claiborne likes to keep busy with business matters, so he keeps a comfortable office on Hamilton Street. He arrives at his office around 9:15 a.m., checks his correspondence, and then reviews his financial information.

He sees appointments or works on his investments, and at 11 a.m. each day he has a relaxing massage given by his long-time masseur and friend, Curtis Jones. "This therapy has contributed much to my well-being over the years," acknowledged Claiborne.

He brought with him his executive assistant, Betty Brown, whom he considered "invaluable" to the Robins family. "She knows just what to do after all these years. I don't know what we'd do without her," he said.

The soft-voiced and efficient Ms. Brown handles his mail, screens his calls and schedules his appointments. He usually sees two or three visitors a week who are seeking gifts to various charitable causes.

"I have a good assistant, everything is in order when I get here, and I stay as a rule 'til about 1:15. And I go home and have a leisurely lunch and read some of the material that I carried home with me, frequently financial things, because I'm interested in investments," Claiborne said.

The lunch waiting for him is prepared by either Lora, or Jean, their housekeeper. "We have a very fine maid that we are very fortunate to have, and she does a good job, but she leaves about 4:30, so she fixes the lunch and cleans the house and does all the things that need to be done.

After lunch he reads until 3:30 p.m., when he takes a nap. "In the afternoon, I rest from about 3:30 'til about 5:30 to 6:00," Claiborne said, "and then I get up feeling renewed and we can go out to dinner or, if we have a social affair, we can go out, but I don't really enjoy social affairs anymore. It takes a lot out of you to be gracious to 100 people," he chuckles.

Nonetheless, social invitations still flood the Robins' mailbox. "I must say, we turn down a lot of them because I just don't have the energy or the strength to pursue an active social life," said Claiborne. "There are some people in this world that are great club people. We belong to all the clubs, the Commonwealth and the Country Club of Virginia, and some people will be over at the Country Club of Virginia three or four nights a week, and that sort of thing.

"I almost never go, mainly because, not that the food is bad, but because when I go over there, there is somebody coming up who hasn't seen me recently who wants to say hello, and you are jumping up and down. I like to go to a restaurant where I can eat undisturbed.

Claiborne and Lora usually go out for dinner once or twice a week. "My wife is an excellent cook, too good — she is a terrific cook — and I would never complain about any of her meals because they are always delicious. But we try to go out so she won't have too much of that," Claiborne said.

"We go to restaurants that maybe a lot of people would think are beneath them, but the food is good. For example, we go to Steak and Ale, best buy in town, frankly. You can get an excellent meal for $10 and I don't know many places you can do that, and we go to places like Red Lobster and Sal Federicos and places like that that we enjoy.

"There is a little Chinese/Polynesian restaurant place out on Patterson Avenue, Tiki Tiki. The food is excellent and they have the best Polynesian drinks. Peter Lee, who heads that, used to be with Trader Vic's in Washington, so he has all the Trader Vic's drink formulas. He makes a perfect Mai Tai," laughs Claiborne.

By spending more time at home, Claiborne keeps an eye on television's "Wall Street Week," and the business news. He and Lora enjoy some of the nightly television shows, and in this manner spend their quiet evenings together. "I don't watch television all the time, as some people do, and yet I suppose, if you really took a timetable of all you watch, you probably watch it more than you think. I watch the sports. I've always been an avid sports fan. I love sports, spectator sports particularly."

In his leisure, Claiborne has plenty of time to reflect on his past. He recalled the insatiable demands of his busy civic life, which are now far behind him. Claiborne no longer pursues the full calendar of meetings that had kept him going day and night as a younger man.

"I try to avoid civic meetings that I used to go to a lot. Betty Brown said that when she first came to work for me she looked at my schedule and she couldn't believe it. It was hectic and it was probably stupid, but I was involved in so many things, and my dear wife put up with it.

"I was gone at least three nights a week, and sometimes four, and tried to be home on weekends. Between one thing and another, I was tied up and I made that choice because, as the head of a company, you were expected to do that if you were going to be a civic leader.

"Maybe I neglected my family to some extent, but bless her heart, she raised them more than I did, but they turned out all right, and they seem to have a great regard for me, so I guess they haven't held it against me too much.

"You make the choice and something has to give, something has to be sacrificed, and hopefully it wasn't too harmful to my family. But it does put the burden on your wife if you are gone a great deal."

Claiborne now finds travel exhausting, and though they still enjoy an annual trip to Florida, only occasionally do they visit his beloved Virginia Beach.

"For many years we went to Virginia Beach, but for the last two or three years we have not gone down there as much. Partly because I'm getting old, I reckon, and battling the traffic, sometimes we just feel like it's not worth it."

Whether for amusement or for a sense of personal independence, Claiborne's main interest in retirement centers on his investments.

"It's a game with me. I could turn it all over to a bank and they could handle it, but that wouldn't be me. I like the challenge of investing, the challenge of outwitting the market, which is, in a sense, what you do. It really is fairly easy to do if you do your homework."

Claiborne's view of the stock market was formed over time, through experience, much like everything else in his life. "There are a few basic principles that if one follows he will do very well, no matter if the market is up or down," explained Claiborne.

"One: Be a fairly long-term investor. Don't go into the market with the idea of buying today and selling next month. You might make a little money that way, but over a period of time, selling and buying, the commissions eat up all your profit. And if you do that, you frequently sell too soon.

"Take a fairly long-term approach, usually five years or more.

However, if the fundamentals start deteriorating, if the earnings start going down, or if the sales start to drop off, or some other catastrophic event happens to the company, you get rid of it quick. One key is to look at the earnings. Have they been going up for ten years?

"I have a number of stocks I have owned for ten to 20 years. The profits have been unbelievable. If a company does well and is continuing to do well, you hold it. You don't get rid of something that is doing well. Many people will take their profits and get out because they are a little afraid, but unless something fundamental has changed, you hang on.

"Two: I tend to look at companies that have paid dividends for at least ten consecutive years and who have increased their dividends. It's not hard to find some good stocks in good industries who have consistently improved sales and increased the dividend every year. I tend to use that as a gauge.

"There are many companies that have increased their dividends for 20 years or more. I do not look at start-up companies, which are very risky. You might make money or you might not.

"Three: Be diversified. You don't put all your eggs in one basket, and you don't invest all your money in one industry. And try to have the top one or two stocks in each industry. For example, you want something in one of the top railroads, two or three of the best utilities, something in manufacturing, one or two in foods, a couple in tobacco, etc. You should have at least two oils, because that is a big industry. You want a broad range so that if one industry gets clobbered for some reason, you are not devastated. By picking the leader such as Coca Cola in the soft drink industry and McDonalds in the fast food industry, you would have made a killing.

"I get a dozen or so stock investment publications, and each cost $100 or so a year, and so for $1,200 I get the advice of a number of people. If you find that a number are recommending the same stock, it usually indicates that there is good sponsorship, people are being encouraged to buy, and there is pressure for it to move up. That doesn't always work, though.

"I agree with one theory about investing in stocks. That is that no matter how much you study or how good your advice, you will win only two-thirds of the time. The interesting thing about the two-thirds theory is that the stocks that go on to perform well do so much better than the ones that do badly. So you really get more than a two-thirds percentage.

"You have to do your homework. You don't just buy because you got a tip. Do your homework and find out what the fundamentals are. And use your own common sense. If in your own town you see a company that is doing well, it's worth investigating.

"Dollar averaging is another method. It means that you put a certain amount of money in a stock each year. That might be a good idea, because if the stock happens to be down on the date that you've set, you get more shares. If the stock is up, you get fewer shares, but over the long-term, dollar averaging is a very good way to invest.

"One way to do that is through what is called the DRIP plan. It's a dividend reinvestment plan, and if you put your quarterly earnings back into the stock, you get the benefit of the so-called dollar averaging.

"Nobody is smart enough to know what is the high for the year or what is the low, and by having a set plan in advance, you are more or less forced to invest on those dates. That's a good plan, particularly for new investors.

"I don't invest in speculative stocks as a general rule. I would rather make a little less money and be in something that's got a record. I don't go to the brokerage houses. They are in business to sell stocks. I might listen to a recommendation, but I'll do the homework on it to decide whether or not to buy it.

"Buying stocks at a low point is called bottom fishing. It can be risky, and yet sometimes it can be very productive. For instance, during the period of the banking crisis, all of the banking stocks dropped, including those of the top banks in the country. You would have thought every bank in the country was going broke based on the price of the stock.

"I bought a lot of bank stocks during that period and made money. But the reason that bottom fishing is a little risky is that there may be something fundamentally wrong with the company, and the stock may go down further. One has to be awfully careful.

"I've stayed out of the automobile stocks, they are so up and down. You may make money on automobile stocks, but I'd rather stay with stocks that have a ten-year up record. Some would disagree with me, of course.

"I would have no more than ten percent in foreign stocks.

And other than my home in Richmond and the one in Virginia Beach, I don't own any real estate. A lot of money has been made in real estate in past years, but I have never been a real estate person.

"If you are in a very high bracket, tax-exempt bonds are very attractive. For example, if you buy a 6¼ percent bond due in 20 years — a Virginia bond — the return on that tax exempt bond is equivalent to more than ten percent on a taxable bond, if you calculate state and federal tax.

"I think most everybody can make money in the stock market if they study the companies, study the earnings, and the progress of the company over the past ten years, and get the top two companies in the industry.

"It's easy to win in stocks because if you can win two out of three times, which you can, you'll be ahead of the game. Nothing you do in life is going to be 100 percent, but if you can be right two-thirds of the time you'll be way, way ahead of the game.

"I tend to make quick decisions. Over the years I found that the quick decisions have been the right ones. If you want to do something, do it now, don't wait. Some people call it hasty, but I think in 99 times out of 100 over my life that my first decision was the best.

"So many decisions in life are not made because there is a risk, but I've found that everything in life is a risk. People who are afraid to take a risk rarely get anywhere. Anybody who is afraid to risk anything doesn't make any money.

XIV

RUMINATIONS ON THE GOLDEN RULE

Those who regard E. Claiborne Robins with great respect and esteem are legion. They are his friends and associates, his employees at A. H. Robins, and the thousands whose lives he has touched through the University of Richmond and a hundred other causes to which he's contributed.

In the spring 1994 issue of the *University of Richmond Magazine,* Claiborne is headlined in a feature article titled: "The Magnificent Giver." His philanthropy is compared to Walter H. Annenberg, John W. Kluge, Paul Mellon and Andrew Carnegie.

"Claiborne Robins is one of those broad-spectrum idealists who can see like realists," printed another local magazine in which Claiborne was featured. "Yet the full extent of his community service is not likely to be disclosed, because of his apparently incurable addiction to anonymity."

Giving without fanfare or popular recognition, Claiborne Robins has been raised to an almost saintly status in the minds and hearts of those closest to him.

Among those are his wife, Lora: "I've never heard anyone ever criticize Claiborne. There's just not another one like him on any level. He has been so good to me, the family and anyone with whom he comes in contact."

University of Richmond President, Dr. E. Bruce Heilman stated: "To me Claiborne Robins is the broad gauge person who is perceptive, dreams dreams, his heart reaches out to people. He is generous to the servant level, to the worker level, to the black community. Claiborne doesn't have to think diversity, he just thinks humanity. I have been refreshed by his goodwill and friendship on every occasion of association."

His lifelong friend, Mary Tyler Cheek, who was often chosen

to make the remarks on occasions to honor Claiborne, described his life, his character, and his generosity best.

"He is a prince of philanthropy. Others have given large gifts but no one in this community has ever been as generous as Claiborne. It has a wonderful quality of magic, like a fairy tale. It's the great American story. It's somebody who begins with a very little and rises to the very top of his chosen field. That gives everyone hope that maybe they too can be successful, and that's a gift in itself."

"Mary Tyler Cheek has always been a good friend," Claiborne said. "I'm a tremendous admirer of her. She always seems to come up with exactly the right theme or toast. When she writes a letter — some of the most beautiful letters that you could ever imagine anybody writing — she seems to be able to come up with just the right word, the right terminology, which is a great gift. I guess she inherited that from her father, Douglas Southall Freeman."

Success is a word often associated with Claiborne for the great personal strides he made throughout his life. Apart from building a billion dollar company from the ground up and his unparalleled philanthropy, Claiborne's success is best measured in terms of his humanity.

The personal relationships he cultivated and the examples he gave others are rooted in a code of ethical conduct so deeply ingrained in him that his every action has been ruled by it. What amounts to a religious devotion, Claiborne prefers to call "the golden rule."

Stated in the New Testament of the Bible, that rule instructs: "So whatever you wish that men would do to you, do so to them; for this is the law and the prophets." For Claiborne, that law has always been first and foremost in his mind and heart, and it has served as the underpinning for his personal religion.

"I believe that the greatest religion is not necessarily going to church every Sunday, but it's one who lives a life more or less based on the golden rule. It sounds rather corny, I know, but let's face it, if you live by the golden rule and treat other people the way you'd like to be treated, you can't go too far wrong. I guess that's my religion.

"I do consider that it is important from the standpoint of how you lead your life, and I think if you lead your life in accordance with the principles that the good Lord apparently set down, the golden rule ... I try every day at least to make at least one person happier than they were the day before. It's fairly easy to do, even without a conscious effort. What a world this would be if everybody did one thing a day to make somebody feel a little happier.

"I like to think that I have, over the years, conducted my life that way, either through charitable contributions or personal words of encouragement, or a letter of congratulations. I've had so many people say to me how much a smile meant. Most people don't realize how important a smile is. My religion, I like to think, is my own behavior in life."

Claiborne has applied the golden rule to all aspects of his life, particularly his management style at the A. H. Robins Company. For this he was considered by his employees to be the best CEO they could ever hope to work for.

Vangie Windsor, a 41 year employee recalled: "I can remember one night up on the 6th floor. It was right after one of the annual reports had just been published, and Mr. Robins came out, and we were looking at the subsidiaries on the back of it, and I said, 'Did you ever in your wildest imagination ever think the company would grow like this?' and he said, 'No,' and you know, tears just started streaming down his cheeks. To me he is still a very humble man. He has always been willing to say, 'I couldn't have done it without you.'"

Georgette Tignor another long term employee recalled: "I fell outside coming to work one morning — late as usual — and broke my kneecap, and Mrs. Robins was one of the first ones to the hospital. They sent me flowers and she was there to see me the very next day. My mother died two days before Christmas and they were right there at the funeral home. They were always faithful to the older people, the ones who started with them. They've really been good to me. I'd have walked over hot coals had they asked me."

"I was always quoted as being paternalistic," said Claiborne, "and I was, but that kind of accusation never bothered me in the slightest, because it worked. I mean, the fact that we took our employees on trips around different places was the most electrifying thing in the world, and no other company in the country was doing it at the time, and they are probably not doing it since. No other company in the world would take them on trips and give them money for spending money — no other company.

"We started the Friday afternoons off with no curtailment of pay. We were the first company in Richmond to start that. You encourage employees and make it worth their while to produce. We recognized outstanding performance.

"One of the secrets of our company was that we adopted the other side of the desk attitude. If I were sitting on the other side of the desk, what would I like to have done? People like to be recognized. We made every effort to do that. I used to call up people on their five-, ten- or 15-year anniversaries just to tell them I hadn't forgotten them."

Claiborne's personal touch created a loyal following of employees who shared his commitment to A. H. Robins, a commitment based on trust and the pursuit of long-term goals. In this, Claiborne's management style was far different from what he sees as the current trend in most U.S. corporations.

"U.S. corporations have this quarterly report syndrome. They feel like they've got to make this quarter look good even if it hurts down the road, because they can't afford to have the stock go down three points. If we had a longer term approach, and if we did not have unions — I think unions are one of the worst things that afflicts the American economy.

"If you notice, every industry that's in serious trouble is heavily unionized, and that's one reason they are so bad for the country. Way back yonder, when employees were taken advantage of, I'm sure unions were a good thing — but they have gotten very powerful, even though they are losing members now. I think they have outlived their usefulness, because most companies know that you cannot operate a business today and have no fringe benefits. If you don't have any fringe benefits no one would come to work for you.

"So the competition assures that most of the things that the unions claim they got, they would have gotten anyway, just as in our own company. We were always one step ahead of the unions. I'm sure they thought about organizing us. The only time we were ever tested was when we bought a company in New Jersey — Elkins Sinn — which was an injectable company.

"The union moved in on us within a few weeks of our buying it, before we had even time to know the employees, and that's why they did it, because they wanted to get to 'em before they got to know us. Well, what we did, since we had a reputation of taking folks on trips — the union couldn't claim it was an unfair labor practice because we'd done it all along — so we just brought all, the whole shebang from Cherry Hills, for three days.

"We just shut up shop up there and brought 'em down here and entertained 'em royally, and we said to them, in effect, 'We are a good company to work for, and if you don't believe it, just talk, ask anybody in the company. Go into the shipping department — anywhere you want to go. Talk to anybody in the company. Find out, is this a good company to work for?' I said, 'We believe in taking care of our employees and doing unto them as we would have it done unto us.' I said, 'Ask about our fringe benefits. Ask about our pension plan.'

"They went back to Cherry Hills and took a vote. It came in — I think it was nearly three-to-one against the union. We found out they had organized a few employees. I got word that one of them was a union person. I made it a point to sit next to her," he laughs. "And she was pretty skeptical at first. I started telling her about things at the company and, before she left here, she had been convinced. We were not unionized."

To long-time Robins employee Johnny Gordon, Claiborne's approach to people has been one of his most endearing traits. "I guess one of the impressive things about Mr. Robins was, and still is, his constant affirmation that people are the company's most valuable assets," said Johnny Gordon.

"I think all of us felt it was our company, even before it went public in 1963, but, of course, when it did go public we were given an opportunity to buy stock and all the employees latched onto that opportunity. They had that much faith in the company."

That faith was engendered by Claiborne, who touched many lives with his thoughtful, genteel mannerisms and natural grace. His attention to detail and courtesy were prompted by a rare sensitivity to others.

"Just think of how many persons you can affect over 80 years or so," remarked Claiborne. "You don't realize in life how you touch lives until something like this happens: I had someone say to me recently that I had written him a letter 25 years ago. He kept the letter and every now and then pulls it out and reads it.

"I get stopped on the street and someone will say that I said something to them when we first met years ago and they've never forgotten it. You don't realize what an impact it is to write a small note or see someone on the street and say something pleasant. It means more than you think."

The cumulative effect of Claiborne's goodwill over the years may be seen in the rapport he has achieved with diverse social, cultural and religious groups.

"I feel equally that every other denomination is worthy, and I'm certainly not what you call a hard shell Baptist. I guess I'd be considered a liberal Baptist. I don't go to church regularly in my later years, but I do support my church generously, and just because I don't go doesn't mean I cut down my contributions, because I do believe in organized religion.

"I believe in the Almighty. I am a Baptist by inheritance. My father was a Baptist and my grandfather was a Baptist. He was one of the founders of the Second Baptist Church. We lived at one time not far from Second Baptist, and I, for many years, went to Sunday school and church, and later on in life, I joined River Road Baptist and I have been a Baptist because, more or less, I fell into it.

"I consider myself religious in the sense that I like to think that I have made this a slightly better world than it was when I came into it, as small as it may be. All of these things have religious overtones. In other words, it makes no difference to me whether someone is Baptist, Presbyterian, Catholic, Jewish.

"Some people have told me — I don't know whether or not it is true — that I'm the most admired person in the Jewish community because I've supported Jewish causes over the years. The fact that I served on several boards that were Jewish-controlled institutions, I probably know as many people in the Jewish community as I do in the gentile community.

"The Jewish people, if you know them, are the most generous — they really support causes they believe in. Some of the largest supporters at the U of R are Jewish. None of the people have any connection with the university — they aren't graduates — they just believe in what we're trying to do."

Claiborne's own generosity has been equally universal. Though his gift to the University of Richmond is his most noted contribution because of its size, his broad range of interests has opened many doors, and it is this broad-range focus he wishes for others.

"The thing that amazes me is that people are so one-sided," remarked Claiborne. "I know people who are at the church three or four nights a week doing something. Now, this is not to be looked down upon, because they are doing worthy work, but imagine having such a narrowed interest that you spend that much time that you don't have time to do anything else.

"That's the thing that I think hopefully distinguishes me. While I've devoted many hours to the university, and that's what's gotten the publicity, I've devoted many, many hundreds of thousands of hours, I guess, to other causes besides the university."

Claiborne is grateful for the opportunity to give, and he values his success in business for that reason far more than amassing personal wealth.

"I think one of the greatest joys of being successful is not necessarily to make a lot of money, because, as I have said many times in my life, over and over again, you can only eat three meals a day if you are prudent. You can't drive more than two cars. You can't legally have but one wife. Beyond living comfortably, which a great many Americans do, and have nice things to put on the table, and to live in a nice home and so forth, beyond that, a lot of wealth means very little, at least to me.

"Except for one thing: it has enabled me to do a lot of good for a lot of different worthy causes, and I think that's one of the joys of wealth. It makes it possible for you to do a lot of good if you are so inclined. Now, I realize that not everybody who has money is so inclined, but as one who has always tried to give over 50 percent of what he earns to charity, I feel that that's been the joy of my life, and I don't think that is so unusual, because there are a lot of people of means who have been very generous.

"I mean the Rockefellers. Look what they have done. Things like colonial Williamsburg, for example. Hadn't been for the Rockefellers, it never would have happened. So many of the museums: the Mellons and thousands of other families have made these substantial contributions to the arts, to cultural benefits, to education. Most private universities could not have survived over the past 30 years if it hadn't been for generous donations from people of some means.

"That is a point that I would like to stress. Success is very satisfying, of course, but the real benefit is to be able to do some of the things that you know you would like to do. I think a person that does not have the means misses a lot of joy in life because they are not able to do these things, and this is what's wrong with the socialist and the communist systems, which have proven to be totally a failure, is that nobody ever has any money to do any of these things. They try to put everybody on the same level, and, as a result, nobody has any money."

Claiborne's political leanings follow the dictates of his conscience and the scope of his experience. As a result, he has achieved a balanced ideology that is not always bound by political party lines.

"I've always considered myself a moderate conservative. I'm certainly not what I would call a hard core conservative, but I am not certainly a liberal. I have found that most liberals are people who are very liberal with other people's money.

"I don't vote necessarily Republican in the state elections. I have voted Democratic, and I have voted Republican, so I'm somewhat of an independent, but I lean to the Republicans because they normally have been a little bit more conservative and a little less the tax-and-spend variety.

"We are seeing right now, in the current Clinton administration, very heavy taxation for those who have been successful and not nearly the amount of spending cuts that were originally promised. They originally promised two-for-one spending cuts for every dollar of taxes. Now it's down to 63 cents of spending cuts for every dollar of taxes, so they have cut it down almost 150 percent from what they said during the campaign, but that is fairly typical of the Democrats. They don't mind socking the taxpayer, at least the National Democratic Party. I believe that it's a mistake to, so-called, sock it to the rich, because they are the people who create jobs and make the donations."

Fluctuations of political power have never distracted Claiborne from his own purpose, which has always been based on long-term goals and a long-term vision. Even in his 80s, Claiborne looked into the future, which was a lesson his grandfather, Albert Hartley Robins, instilled.

"I don't consider that age is a matter of years. I've known a few people who were close to 90 that were about as young as, in fact younger, than some people who were 25. It's an outlook on life. I remember my grandfather ... one thing I remember about him when he was up over 90 and bedridden, he was always thinking about what he was going to do in the next five years.

"I never heard him once look back. He was always planning what he hoped to accomplish. Well, now, if you can get a 90-year-old thinking along those lines, he's going to be young. Most people, when they get to be old, they tend to look back and think of the past, but they don't maintain a youthful approach.

"I think one of the great things about youth is that, if a person is ambitious, particularly, they are always planning what they are going to do and how they are going to make a greater success. I think it ties into health, too. I think a person who is optimistic and who is looking ahead, looking forward, and planning, and staying busy doing that, as a rule has better health. Because nothing kills people quicker than worry."

Claiborne's natural optimism and good nature have always prevailed. Even during the dark days of the Dalkon Shield, Claiborne held to his buoyant optimism.

"I have always been a person for whom the glass has always been half full, not half empty. It's so stupid to let things that you can't control worry you too much. If you can't do anything about it, what good will it do to worry about it? And it affects your health. I don't think anything affects your health more than worry. I've never been a worrier, because I think that if you have faith in the Lord and try to do what's right, things will turn out all right.

"The mind has a tremendous influence over the health of an individual, and if you can stay optimistic, even when things aren't going well, you're going to be in a lot better health, I think. And sometimes, I think that is even greater than any medicine.

"I hate to put that in a book, but I guess that's true. In looking back over my life, when times were the roughest and everything looked like it was going wrong, almost without exception it has turned out to be a good thing in the long run. There was a light at the end of the tunnel, and there was sunshine the next day, and so forth."

Healthy moderation is another of Claiborne's rules of thumb. Claiborne explains, "I never worry about all these things I am always reading about: 'This is bad for you and this is bad for you and this is bad for you.' I don't ever cut out any of these things that are bad for you. I don't eat an egg every day 'cause I know it's loaded with cholesterol, but other than a few moderate changes like that, I eat pretty much what I want.

"The secret there is moderation: don't eat too much of anything. If everything is so bad for you, why are we all living longer? That's my philosophy. My goodness, if you gave up everything that's supposedly not good for you, you wouldn't have a great variety to eat."

Worry might not be a predominant part of Claiborne's life, but he does have concerns about the future of the pharmaceutical industry. Over the years, Claiborne has championed the industry because of its susceptibility to criticism, government control and litigation.

"I am concerned about the future of the industry because the drug industry is so vulnerable. In the first place, there are not many voters. It's a relatively small group. They are not politically powerful, and people who are cutting costs don't ever seem to care about whether research is stifled.

"It now costs around $200 to $300 million to get a new drug approved because of the severe and long testing required by the FDA. Now, no company in their right mind is going to invest $200 million unless they think they can get it back, and I'm afraid what's going to happen under the worst scenario is that research will be stifled and developments in the future will be limited, and the American people will suffer.

"There are a lot of people who are heading pharmaceutical companies today who really don't know much about the pharmaceutical business, strangely enough. They are lawyers or they are financial people, they are corporate executives who have been promoted up the line, but they really don't know an awful lot. They are not pharmacists. I think I was, at the time — and it is even more true today — I was the only pharmacist that was ever chairman of the PMA.

"I've just done something yesterday (March 9, 1993) that may or may not be significant, but I made a gift of $125,000 to the American Pharmaceutical Association to challenge retail pharmacists in the country, who are members of the American Pharmaceutical Association, and manufacturers, to come up with funds to present to the American public why drugs cost what they do. If we can get the support of the manufacturers and the pharmacists, the APA could say things that the manufacturers couldn't very well say because they would be considered prejudiced.

"Somebody had to start it and they approached me as to whether I would be willing to consider this and I acted favorably on it. I said I couldn't carry the load, but I'd certainly start it off with a challenge gift.

"There are very good reasons why drugs cost what they do today, and the fact that we are all living so much longer is directly attributable to ... now doctors, and, of course, hospitals have made progress, but if they didn't have these new drugs that are really miraculous ... just as my father died when he was very young because there was nothing available to treat him. Today, he would be cured in a flash.

"What people forget is the life expectancy, how much better it is now than it was even when my father was born. I believe it was in the 40s, was life expectancy."

Given his political stance and his familiarity with medicine,

Claiborne has expressed strong opinions about the health care reform effort launched by the Clinton administration in the early 1990s.

"Certainly, it's a desirable objective to have universal health care for those that can't afford it," allowed Claiborne. "But in order to get universal care, you've got to put ceilings on what a doctor or what a hospital can charge. A hospital has certain expenses that go on no matter what, and you start putting ceilings on hospital costs ... you may be able to do to a limited degree, but when you clamp down too hard, the hospital is going to go out of business, and then you're not going to have a hospital.

"Maybe there are too many hospitals, I don't know, but I'm concerned that what we'll get is kind of a socialized medicine set up not unlike what they have in England. But what has happened there, because the participants feel like it's free, it has just placed an enormous burden on the health care system.

"In other words, you go to see a doctor there, there might be a hundred people ahead of you, waiting. Because what people do is, if they have an ache or a pain, they go to see the doctor. Maybe if they had to pay for it they'd decide the ache wasn't so bad and the pain wasn't so bad.

"It's a lot easier to save than to cut these costs. I will be amazed if they are able to cut them as much as they think they will. They claim it will cost up to $90 billion a year to give health care to everybody. Now, where are you are going to get $90 billion? They are either going to put more and more taxes to cover it, or you're going to squeeze the health system so from the top that it is going to effect the quality and availability for the patient.

"One of the greatest things they could do is to put a limit on liability. There has been some effort in that direction, but not very successful, because lawyers control the legislators. But they could put a $250,000 cap on liability, no matter what it is, then the doctors wouldn't run 20 extra tests to protect themselves against liability, and that would cut down a lot of costs."

RUMINATIONS ON THE GOLDEN RULE

Claiborne's willingness to suggest reform measures illustrates his openess to constructive ideas and their sometimes risky implementaion. Rather than fearing failure in any segment of his life, Claiborne has always made an effort.

"I think failure is not bad if you learn from it," he said. "I've been fortunate in my life in that I haven't had many failures. I'm sure everybody has some. If you learn from it and prove yourself because of it, then you are probably ahead."

Trusting his intuition and the guidance of his conscience, Claiborne has sometimes followed the path less traveled. Conformity rarely influenced him as he followed his inner guide.

"The interesting thing about my life, and I suspect it is true of most people's lives, is that if you had to do it all over again, you probably wouldn't do too many things differently. Oh, sure, there'd be a spot here and a spot there that you would have done a little bit differently.

"I've been fortunate, of course, and I've had a very gratifying life in that it has been fulfilling, and I feel like I've helped a lot of people, not only in creating jobs, but hopefully enabling them to enjoy their job and be a contributing citizen to the community.

"I guess what startles me, looking back on it, I started out with $2,000 and no capital to speak of. Other than that, it never dawned on me that I could fail. I guess it was youth. The thought of failing never entered my mind. I was so sure."

"I've been so blessed. I have never been bored in my life. I've been busy since I was old enough to sell newspapers and I'm still busy in retirement. I've had an exciting 84 years."

CHRONOLOGY

1842 - Albert Hartley Robins is born
1866 - Albert Hartley Robins opens his apothecary on 523 North Second
       Street in Richmond, Virginia
1891 - Albert moves his apothecary to 200 E. Marshall Street
1896 - Claiborne Robins founds the A. H. Robins Company and intro-
       duces ROBINS CASCARA COMPOUND
1910 - E. Claiborne Robins is born
1912 - Claiborne Robins dies at age 39 and Martha Taylor Robins takes
       over the business
1929 - A. H. Robins Company moves to 5 South Sixth Street
1933 - E. Claiborne Robins joins the A. H. Robins Company with sales
       of $4800
1934 - Albert Hartley Robins dies at age 92
1934 - E. Claiborne Robins introduces DONNATAL, THEORATE, and
       BIRONEX
1936 - E. Claiborne Robins becomes President and CEO of A. H. Robins
       Company
1938 - E. Claiborne Robins marries Lora E. McGlasson of Waco, Texas
1940 - E. Claiborne and Lora's first child, Lora Elizabeth is born
1942 - Sales reach $100,000
1943 - E. Claiborne and Lora's second child, E. Claiborne Jr. is born
1943 - A. H. Robins moves to 12 South Twelfth Street
1945 - Claiborne and Lora's third child, Ann Carol is born
1948 - A. H. Robins moves to 1322 West Broad Street
1948 - Sales reach one million dollars
1949 - ROBITUSSIN, PABALATE and ENTOZYME are introduced
1950 - A. H. Robins rents additional space at 1711 Ellen Rd
1953 - A. H. Robins corporate headquarters at 1407 Cummings Dr. is built
1956 - DIMETANE is licensed from Schering
1957 - Martha Taylor Robins dies at age 74
1958 - A. H. Robins Company Limited is established in the U.K.
1961 - Claiborne and Lora's first grandchild, Juliet Elizabeth Shield,
       is born to daughter Elizabeth
1963 - Robins Research Center is built
1963 - Morton Manufacturing Corporation is purchased and
       CHAP STICK is acquired

CHRONOLOGY

1963 - A. H. Robins goes public and is traded OTC

1963 - Sales reach 50 million dollars

1964 - Sanicol, S.A. of Bogota, Colombia is purchased

1965 - A. H. Robins is listed on the New York Stock Exchange

1966 - E. Claiborne Robins, Jr. joins A. H. Robins

1966 - Laboratoires Martinet S.A. of Dreux, France is purchased

1967 - Polk Miller Products Corporation is purchased and the SERGEANT'S line of pet care products is acquired

1967 - Parfums Caron is purchased

1970 - E. Claiborne Robins becomes Chairman of the Board of A. H. Robins

1970 - Manufacturing plant is built

1970 - E. Scheurich Pharmwerk GmbH of Baden, West Germany is purchased

1973 - VioBin Corporation of Monticello, IL is purchased

197? - Elkins-Sinn, Inc. of Cherry Hill, NJ is purchased

1975 - A. H. Robins (Schweiz) GmbH is established in Zug, Switzerland

1975 - E. Claiborne Robins steps down as CEO but retains the position of Chairman of the Board

1975 - William Zimmer, III takes over CEO position

1977 - Sales reach 300 million dollars

1978 - E. Claiborne Robins, Jr. takes over position of President and CEO

1979 - Georg A. Brenner Arzneimittel-Fabrik GmbH of Alpirsbach, Schwarzwald, West Germany is purchased

1980 - A. H. Robins Darbytown Road production plant is built

1980 - Kytta-Werk Sauter GmbH of Alpirsbach, Schwarzwald, West Germany is purchased

1982 - Willows Francis veterinary business is purchased in the U.K. and merges with A. H. Robins Company Limited

1983 - Sales reach 500 million dollars

1984 - Quinton Instrument Company of Seattle, WA is purchased

1985 - A. H. Robins Pty. Limited is established in Canterbury, New South Wales, Australia

1985 - A. H. Robins Company files for bankruptcy protection under chapter 11

1989 - E. Claiborne Robins retires from A. H. Robins Company

1989 - American Home Products Corporation purchases A. H. Robins Company for approximately 3.4 billion dollars

1995 - E. Claiborne Robins dies on July 6

Additional Domestic Subsidiaries

Agri-Bio Corp., Gainesville, GA

A. H. Robins International Company, Las Vegas, NV

A. H. Robins Manufacturing Company, Arecibo, Puerto Rico
Eurand America, Incorporated, Dayton, OH
Lee Laboratories, Inc., Petersburg, VA
Mil-Mor Media, Incorporated, Richmond, VA
Robins Communications, Inc., Greensboro, NC
U.S. Clinical Products, Inc., Richardson, TX

Additional Foreign Subsidiaries
Canada
A. H. Robins Canada Inc., Mississauga, Ontario, Canada

Latin America
A. H. Robins International, S.A., Bogota, Colombia
Industrial Santa Agape, S.A., Guatemala City, Guatemala
A. H. Robins de Mexico, S.A., Cuautitlan, Mexico
Industrias Galmex, S.A., Cuautitlan, Mexico
Laboratorios Ergos, S.A., Caracas, Venezuela

Europe
Eurand France S.A., Creil, France
Medipha S.A., Dreux, France
Eurand Italia S.p.A., Milan, Italy
Eurand International S.r.l., Milan, Italy
A. H. Robins Farmaceutica, S.A., Madrid, Spain
Diffucap-Eurand S.A., Stabio, Switzerland
Eurand Microencapsulation S.A., Stabio, Switzerland

Middle East & Africa
A. H. Robins International Company**, Athens, Greece
A. H. Robins International Company**, Tehran, Iran
A. H. Robins (Iran) Company, Tehran, Iran
A. H. Robins Company (South Africa)(Proprietary) Limited,
Johannesburg, South Africa

Far East
A. H. Robins International Company**, Taipei, Taiwan
A. H. Robins International Company**, Tokyo, Japan
American Drug Corporation, Tokyo, Japan
A. H. Robins (Philippines) Company, Inc., Pasig, Metro Manila,
Philippines

Honors and Affiliations

Professional and Social Affiliations

Past President - Better Business Bureau of Richmond (1956)
Past President - Medical College of Virginia Alumni Association
Past President - Richmond Baseball, Inc.
Past President - Richmond Chamber of Commerce (1952)
Past President - University of Richmond Alumni Council

Past Chairman - Board of Directors, Pharmaceutical Manufacturers
Association (Member of the Board 1965-1976)

Trustee Emeritus - University of Richmond
Trustee Emeritus - Richmond Memorial Hospital

Honorary Member - Board of Trustees, Children's Hospital,
Richmond, Virginia

Co-Chairman - Richmond Committee for Hampton Institute - 1967

Charter Member - Downtown Development Unlimited, Richmond, Virginia

Past Director - The Chesapeake and Potomac Telephone Company
of Virginia

Past Director - Ethyl Corporation
Past Director - Richmond Corporation
Past Director - Life Insurance Company of Virginia
Past Director - Virginia Electric and Power Company
Past Director - Central Fidelity Bank, N.A.
Past Director - Thalhimer Brothers, Inc.

Member - Commonwealth Club, Richmond
Member - Country Club of Virginia, Richmond
Member - Delta Zeta Chapter of Alpha Kappa Psi (Commerce) at the
University of Richmond (Honorary)
Member - Forum Club, Richmond
Member - Kappa Psi Pharmaceutical Fraternity (Social)

Member - Lambda Chi Alpha Fraternity (Initiated as Honorary Member,
    April 1959)
Member - Medical College of Virginia Alumni Association (Served on
    Board for four years)
Member - Newcomen Society of North America
Member - Phi Beta Kappa Fraternity
Member - Omicron Delta Kappa Fraternity (Honorary)
Member - Phi Delta Chi fraternity (Honorary)
Member - Delta Theta Phi (Honorary)
Member - Richmond Rotary Club (Served as Director for four years;
    named Honorary Life Member 1990)
Member - Virginia Pharmaceutical Association (Honorary Life
    membership conferred in June 1969)
Member - Richmond Council, Navy League of the United States

Honorary Charter Member - Beta Gamma Sigma, University of Richmond

Honorary Degree - Doctor of Pharmaceutical Science, conferred by the
    Medical College of Virginia in 1958
Honorary Degree - Doctor of Laws, conferred by the University of
    Richmond in 1960
Honorary Degree - Doctor of Science in Pharmacy, conferred by the
    Massachusetts College of Pharmacy and Allied Health
    Sciences in 1969 Virginia Union University
    in May 1980

Honored by the Newcomen Society of North America at a dinner in
    Richmond on May 19, 1966
Honored by the University of Richmond, which renamed its School of
    Business the E. Claiborne Robins School of Business of the
    University of Richmond, September 5, 1979
Honored by the School of Pharmacy of the Medical College of Virginia,
    which established the E. Claiborne Robins Distinguished
    Professorship, March 1988

Award - Distinguished Service Award, presented by the University of
    Richmond, 1960
Award - Pharmacist of the Year, presented by the Virginia Pharmaceutical
    Association, 1967
Award - Dean M. McCann Award for Distinguished Service, presented by
    the Pharmaceutical Wholesalers Association, 1968

Honors and Affiliations

Award - Hugo H. Schaefer Medal, presented by the American
Pharmaceutical Association, May 1969

Award - Business Leader of the Year, presented by the Sales and
Marketing Executives of Richmond, November 1969

Award - Liberty Bell Award, presented by the Richmond Bar Association,
April 1970

Award - Service to Mankind Award, presented by the Sertoma Club of
Richmond, June 1970

Award - Thomas Jefferson Award for Public Service, presented by the Old
Dominion Chapter, Public Relations Society of America,
September 1970

Award - Medallion of Honor, presented by the Virginians of Maryland,
January 1971

Award - National Honoree, Beta Gamma Sigma, May 1971

Award - Distinguished Service Award, presented by the Virginia State
Chamber of Commerce, May 1972

Award - Jackson Davis Award for Distinguished Service to Higher
Education in Virginia, presented by the Virginia Conference of
the American Association of University Professors, April 1976

Award - Cultural Laureate Award in Commerce, presented by the Virginia
Cultural Laureate Foundation, September 1977

Award - Edward A. Wayne Medal for Distinguished Service, presented by
Virginia Commonwealth University, May 1978

Award - Hall of Fame Award for Exceptional Contribution to Sports,
presented by the Virginia Sports Hall of Fame, November 1979

Award - Named to the University of Richmond's Athletic Hall of Fame,
April 1990

Award - Great American Traditions Award, presented by B'nai B'rith
International, June 1982

Award - Outstanding Alumnus Award, presented by the Pharmacy
Division of the Medical College of Virginia Alumni Association of
Virginia Commonwealth University, February 1983

Award - The University of Richmond's Paragon Medal, presented to
individuals who have rendered uncommon and generally
unparalleled service to the University, not awarded to a
subsequent recipient during the lifetime of the honoree
and not awarded more frequently than every fifteen years,
May 1986

Award - Alumnus of the Year Award, presented by the Medical College of
Virginia Alumni Association of Virginia Commonwealth
University, May 1986

Award - Distinguished Citizens Award, Robert E. Lee Council, Boy
Scouts of America, December 1991

An Angel on my Shoulder

Award - Honorary President of the American Pharmaceutical Association
    1992/1993
Award - Alexis de Tocqueville Society Award, United Way Services'
    highest honor for Volunteerism, September 199

A family portrait taken on the occasion of the Boy Scout Dinner, December, 1991.
Left to right front row: Robert E. Marchant, Ann Carol Robins Marchant, Erin Hartley Robins,
Lora McGlasson Robins, Mark Claiborne Robins, Elizabeth Robins Porter, Juliet Elizabeth Shield,
J. David Taylor. Back row: Christopher Robins Haskell, Gregory Christopher Robins, Susan P.
Robins, Sheryl Ann Robins, E. Claiborne Robins, Jr., Mary Ellen W. Robins, E. Claiborne Robins,
John Tariot, Robin Richardson Shield, Robert E. Porter.

A. H. Robins Products (1930s-1989)

ADABEE — Vitamins

ALLBEE (and family) — B Complex Vitamins

AMBAR (and family) — Methamphetamine with Phenobarbital

ARTHRALGEN — Antirheumatic-Analgesic

BIRONEX (formerly **BIRON**) — Hematinic; Ferrous sulfate

CAMPETRODIN — Antiseptic dressing of iodine and oil

CHAP STICK — Lip Balm

COUGH CALMERS — Expectorant-Antitussive

DALKON SHIELD — Intrauterine Device

DIMACOL — Antitussive-Decongestant-Expectorant

DIMETANE (and family) — Antihistamine

DIMETAPP — Antihistamine-Decongestant

DONNA EXTENTABS — Belladonna Alkaloids with extended action

DONNAGEL — Antidiarrheal; Kaolin and Pectin with belladonna
  alkaloids; -PG contained a Paregoric equivalent

DONNAGESIC — **DONNATAL** plus an analgesic

DONNALATE — Antacid-Antispasmodic-Sedative; **DONNATAL** plus
  ROBALATE

DONNATAL (and family) — Sedative-Antispasmodic; Belladonna
  Alkaloids with Phenobarbital

DONNAZYME — Digestant; **DONNATAL** plus **ENTOZYME**

DOPRAM — Respiratory Stimulant; Doxapram Hydrochloride

ENTOZYME — Digestant

EXNA (and family) — Diuretic; Benzthiazide

H-P-V CAPSULES (formerly **HI-PO-VITA**) — Vitamins

LIP QUENCHER (and family) — Cosmetics

LIP SOOTHER — Lip cream

LIP TREAT — Lip Gloss

MEPHATE — Skeletal Muscle Relaxant and C.N.S. Sedative

MICRO-K — Potassium Chloride

MITROLAN — Laxative-Antidiarrheal; Calcium Polycarbophil

PABALATE (and family)— Antirheumatic

PHENAPHEN (and family) — Analgesic-Sedative; formerly
  Phenacetin with Phenobarbital; changed to Acetaminophen — some
  preparations contained codeine

PONDIMIN — Anorectic; Fenfluramine Hydrochloride

QUINIDEX — Long-acting form of Quinidine Sulfate

REGLAN — Promotes gastric emptying-Antiemetic; Metoclopramide Hydrochloride

ROBALATE — Antacid

ROBAMOX, ROBICILLIN, ROBIMYCIN, ROBITET — Antibiotics

ROBAXIN, ROBAXISAL — Muscle Relaxants; Methocarbamol

ROBINS CASCARA COMPOUND, Mild and Strong — Laxative

ROBINUL (and family) — Anticholinergic

ROBITUSSIN (and family) — Antitussive-Expectorant; some preparations contained a decongestant and/or codeine

SERGEANT'S FLEA AND TICK COLLAR (and family) — Pet Care

SEDOBARB — Sedative-Hypnotic; Phenobarbital with Pentobarbital

SILAIN (and family) — Antacid

TENEX — Anti-hypertensive; Guanfacine Hydrochloride

THEORATE — Diuretic-Cardiovascular Stimulant; Theobromine with Phenobarbital

URALITHIC SALT — Antiseptic

VIOKASE — Digestive

Z-BEC — Vitamins with Zinc